SIX ESSAYS

ON

THE PLATONIC THEORY OF
KNOWLEDGE

SIX ESSAYS

ON

THE PLATONIC THEORY OF KNOWLEDGE

as expounded in the later dialogues and
reviewed by Aristotle

by

MARIE V. WILLIAMS

late Marion Kennedy Student of Newnham College

Cambridge:
at the University Press
1908

CAMBRIDGE
UNIVERSITY PRESS

University Printing House, Cambridge CB2 8BS, United Kingdom

Cambridge University Press is part of the University of Cambridge.

It furthers the University's mission by disseminating knowledge in the pursuit of
education, learning and research at the highest international levels of excellence.

www.cambridge.org
Information on this title: www.cambridge.org/9781107448148

First published 1908
First paperback edition 2014

A catalogue record for this publication is available from the British Library

ISBN 978-1-107-44814-8 Paperback

PREFACE

THE following essays, written during my tenure of a studentship at Newnham College, Cambridge, were the outcome of a genuine interest in the Platonic controversy, and of a desire to satisfy myself, by independent study, regarding the doctrines that the later dialogues seem to teach. In a subject that has for so long been the source of disagreements one can scarcely hope to produce a work that will commend itself to every critic, or to bridge in any degree the chasm that already yawns between the two leading schools of interpretation; and I must own frankly, at once, that I belong to the school that sees in the later work of Plato a fuller development and elaboration of the ideal scheme which was at first but vaguely sketched. It is not the spirit of controversy, however, but the hope for a better understanding of this position on the part of other controversialists, that has led me to publish these papers. In preparing them I have not neglected to make myself acquainted with the position taken by other schools; but that I am chiefly indebted to the Platonic scholars of Cambridge cannot be denied.

A word perhaps should be said in regard to the order in which the Platonic dialogues are here taken. I have assumed throughout—and I believe there is now almost general agreement on this point—that the six dialogues with which I chiefly deal, viz., the *Parmenides*, *Theaetetus*, *Sophist*, *Politicus*, *Philebus* and *Timaeus*, are posterior to the *Republic* and the *Phaedo*, and that, whatever be the order in which they are to be ranked, they belong, roughly speaking, to the same period of Plato's thought. The special order in which they are grouped here was particularly suited to the form of my essays, being based mainly on affinity in subject-matter; and any re-arrangement of the first four would not materially affect any of the conclusions I have reached. The *Philebus* and the *Timaeus*, however, I cannot help regarding for many reasons as posterior to the other four, and I believe that this, too, will be conceded by the majority of scholars. For my own part, I would go further and make the *Timaeus* the latest of them all, though I do not think that this particular article of faith is absolutely essential for the acceptance of the results of my essays. The *Philebus* and the *Timaeus* have so much in common that they must have belonged to practically the same period of Plato's life; and the obscurity of the former might plausibly be assigned either to the initial vagueness of a fresh development in Plato's philosophy, or to the contraction due to recapitulation.

I have derived the greatest benefit from Professor Jackson's articles in the "Journal of Philology", and from Mr Archer-Hind's edition of the *Timaeus*. I have read, too, with great interest various articles by Professor Shorey in the "American Journal of Philology", and others by Mr A. E. Taylor in "Mind". I have profited also from Carlill's lately-published edition of the *Theaetetus* and *Philebus*.

My grateful thanks are due to Mr R. D. Archer-Hind for much kind help and criticism, and also to Dr Budge of the British Museum for various suggestions regarding the subject-matter of Essay V. I must also acknowledge my obligations to Miss Alice Gardner, of Newnham College, and Miss M. E. Thomson, of King's College, Aberdeen, for their help at the proof-correcting stage. Finally, I must thank the officials of the University Press for their courteous assistance in the details of publication.

M. V. W.

ISLEWORTH,
      January 21*st*, 1908.

CONTENTS

ESSAY I.

THE SEARCH FOR KNOWLEDGE.

THE desire for knowledge, so Aristotle[1] tells us, is implanted by nature in all men, but the intensity of the desire varies in different ages, and in different types of men, and in the same men at different stages of their lives. Plato, we know, found in it a motive power that never ceased, throughout a long life, to urge him on to intellectual labour and achievement, but even in his history one may detect times of crisis, in which the fervour of a glorious hope, or a dogged pertinacity in research, shows that he is grappling with the problem in its vastness.

It is in the *Phaedo* and the *Republic*, first of all, that he makes a systematic attempt to formulate a scheme of knowledge. In the former, disappointed by his study of Anaxagoras, he determines to make use of the indirect method of λόγοι, if thereby he may attain to metaphysical verity. In the latter his scheme is complete, his plans are laid, and already he beholds in anticipation the ἰδέα τἀγαθοῦ, which is exalted above both knowledge and being, and is the goal of every

---

[1] *Met.* A. i. 1.

human effort. The last chapters of Book VI reveal the
philosopher's aspiration visualised and glorified, and we
cannot doubt that he has actual and definite hope of
attaining to the truth he is pursuing along the lines
which he there indicates. Yet the dialectical method
of the *Republic* is not of a kind to satisfy either pupils
or master; it is obscured by excess of light: the flights
of imagination have reached a height to which sober
intellect cannot climb. It is imperative, therefore, that
the process of ascent from the assumption of εἴδη to the
attainment of the ἀρχὴ ἀνυπόθετος should be described
in language of scientific precision, and a still μακροτέρα
περίοδος must be undertaken before knowledge is
attainable. It is with some of the sign-posts that mark
off this more circuitous route that the present papers
propose to deal.

It would be as well to have in mind at the outset
the leading features of the metaphysical and dialectical
scheme of the *Republic*, and of its complementary
dialogue, the *Phaedo*, which belongs to the same stage
of Platonic thought, and may perhaps have been written
somewhat earlier.

In the first place we are definitely informed[1] that,
quite apart from the world of sensible things, which,
being subject to the Heracleitean flux, can never be
objects of knowledge, there are certain perfect and
immutable forms, εἴδη αὐτὰ καθ' αὑτά. The exact significance of the phrase αὐτὰ καθ' αὑτά is not easy of
determination, but in the light of Aristotle's[2] evidence
it seems plain that the εἴδη are transcendental unities,

---

[1] *Rep.* 476 A; 596 A; *Phaedo* 100 B seq.
[2] *Met.* A. 987b 7.

exalted in some vague and mysterious way above the world of sensible phenomena by reason of their utter perfection and immobility. The ideas, then, are αὐτὰ καθ᾽ αὑτὰ chiefly in virtue of the sharp contrast drawn between them and material things, for that they had some connexion with one another, and with the idea of Good, is an inevitable consequence of the dialectical scheme propounded in Book VI.

Further, we are told that the things of sense, through μέθεξις in εἴδη, become possessed of certain characteristics, and are called by certain names and described in certain terms, an attempt thereby being made to explain the possibility of predication[1]. Every predicate corresponds to an immutable idea, in which the particular of which it is predicated participates. Here again one is unable to render a satisfactory account of the word μέθεξις. The qualification, ὅπῃ δὴ καὶ ὅπως προσγενομένη, introduced at Phaedo 100 D, certainly shows that the method was but hazily conceived in the mind of Plato himself, and that the import of the word is mainly metaphorical, like that of the kindred term μίμησις, which occurs more frequently, though not exclusively, in the later dialogues[2]. By the very vagueness of its statement the doctrine was assuredly exposed to the literal interpretation which is ridiculed in the Parmenides, but that this interpretation was Plato's deliberate meaning in the Phaedo and the Republic we have no justification for saying.

Such then is the nature of the εἴδη which form the ground-work of the dialectical process of Republic VI,

[1] See Ar. Met. A. 987ᵇ 9, 10.
[2] Cf. Rep. x. 597 seq.

4 THE SEARCH FOR KNOWLEDGE

a process which, in contradistinction to the inferior system of διάνοια, leads directly from the assumption of hypotheses to a first cause of all, and is in no way dependent upon the things of sense. Whereas διάνοια proceeds from the assumption of hypotheses to a conclusion, dialectic proceeds upwards from hypothesis to hypothesis, until the idea of Good, upon which all other ideas depend, is in sight. Once the ἰδέα τἀγαθοῦ is reached, the hypotheses through which it is attained become realities; they are no longer ideas hypothetically asserted but actively realised. The ideas which are thus hypothetically assumed are illustrated chiefly by the universals of mathematics, and one may conclude that it was chiefly through ideas of this nature that Plato thought of rising to a knowledge of the Good; but, on the analogy of the converse process of λόγοι mentioned at *Phaedo* 101 D, and from the fact that ζῷα, φυτευτά, etc., are at 510 B, 511 A said to serve as εἰκόνες in the lower νόησις, one would conclude that other universal hypotheses too, such as the assumption of an αὐτὸ τὸ ζῷον, are conceived of as contributing some share to the realisation of the Good. As to the function of λόγοι, it would appear that a λόγος or definition is the mental or verbal counterpart of the εἶδος whose existence is asserted, and that the λόγοι play an important part in the dialectical process. The first step is to postulate an εἶδος, the next to define it, then, in virtue of the knowledge thus gained, an εἶδος of a yet higher order is postulated until the ἰδέα τἀγαθοῦ is reached. When the ἰδέα τἀγαθοῦ has been defined and grasped, we have not only true knowledge but true being, for in the idea of Good knowledge and

being coincide, and the mere fact of attaining to it has
proved that our λόγοι were correct representatives of
the ideal reality. Thence, as Plato says, the dialectician
may descend with confidence in the line of the εἴδη,
verifying all the assumptions that he originally made;
the ὑποθέσεις have now become ἀρχαὶ in virtue of their
connexion with the ἀρχὴ ἀνυπόθετος.

The system of knowledge, then, as delineated in the
Republic, is at best a sketch. It is shadowy and indefinite, and proclaims itself a product of immature
thought. It shows no comprehension of the essential
differences in general predicates, no consciousness that
some have a relative, others a substantive, significance.
In short, the scheme must not only be re-stated, but
re-thought, before any satisfactory advance can be made;
and before it can be re-stated, or even re-thought, the
whole subject of predication and thought must be
thoroughly analysed, investigated, and systematised.
To this preliminary task Plato addresses himself especially in the *Parmenides, Theaetetus, Sophist* and
Politicus; the greater task of re-thinking and re-
stating his earlier scheme belongs chiefly, though not
exclusively, to the *Philebus* and *Timaeus*. I now propose to deal with some of the most striking contributions
of the *Parmenides, Theaetetus* and *Sophist* to the
logical problem, reserving for further treatment the
constructive results of the *Politicus, Philebus* and
Timaeus.

The first half of the *Parmenides* consists mainly of
an account of the ideal theory of the *Phaedo* and *Republic*, followed by a systematic criticism of the theory
as it was stated in those dialogues. First of all we

remark that the young Socrates, who is introduced as
the exponent of the theory, and of its importance in the
problem of predication, displays considerable aversion
to assuming ideas to correspond to every predicate ;
also that there seems to be a tendency to draw distinctions within the ideal world, and to class certain
ideas together, instead of collecting them under the
heterogeneous category that *Republic* 596 A implies.
Here ideas of qualities, of ethical notions, of natural
species, of meaner objects, are enumerated separately,
as if it were unconsciously felt that they are essentially
distinct from one another.   Socrates, though assenting
cheerfully to the assumption of ideas of qualities and
of ethical notions, seems less convinced of the existence
of ideas of natural kinds, and his whole soul revolts
from the thought of ideas of such things as hair, mud,
dirt: Parmenides, however, rebukes him, on the ground
that such a feeling is unworthy of the true philosopher.
"You are young, Socrates," he says, "and when philosophy has got a firmer hold of you, you will not despise
even the meanest things "—a remark which should be
borne in mind as indicating in general the line of
development which the young Socrates, and Plato,
whom he represents, may be expected to take.

The destructive criticism that follows is well known
to every reader of Plato.   If the particular participates
in the idea, it must participate either in the whole or a
part ; if in the whole, the idea is not one but many ; if
in the part, the idea becomes divided, and is many.
Hence the idea is either not a unity, or else particulars
cannot participate in it.   Furthermore, if every plurality
of particulars called by the same name has an idea

corresponding to it, the idea will be indefinitely multiplied, for the idea when added to the first group constitutes another group, for which another idea must be postulated, and so on *ad infinitum*. These two arguments, it must be noted, are aimed, not so much at the existence of ideas, as against the statements regarding their nature which were made in the *Phaedo* and *Republic*. It is not the existence of ideas, but their supposed actual immanence in particulars, and their intimate connexion with predication, that is chiefly attacked—a conclusion which is confirmed by the further steps of the controversy.

Socrates, to extricate himself from these difficulties, suggests that the fatal consequences might not follow if the idea were conceived of as a νόημα existing only in ψυχαί. Parmenides, however, points out that every νόημα must be supposed to have an object, and that this would only give us the old idea back again, remarking further that such a conception of the idea in no way justifies an inherent connexion between ideas and phenomena. To this Socrates replies, as if by sudden inspiration, that perhaps the connexion is not μέθεξις, after all, but the ideas are to be thought of as παραδείγματα ἑστῶτα ἐν τῇ φύσει, also that particulars partake of ideas in virtue of resemblance and nothing else. But even this brilliant suggestion is of no avail so long as he holds that the predication of likeness involves the existence of an idea, by reason of which the particulars resemble each other and the idea. The infinite regress meets us still, and we have made no progress.

But, says Parmenides, the greatest difficulty of all

is yet to come. If ideas are to be αὐτὰ καθ' αὐτά, separately existent apart from particulars, then they are altogether remote from the sphere of human thought and action, and cannot possibly serve as objects of human knowledge: if they have relations, they are related to one another only, and have no intercourse with the things of sense which are said to resemble them. Yet, without a belief in their existence, what hope is there of attaining to truth? There must be eternal fixities somewhere on which the mind can rest, and before Socrates can hope to attack so great a dilemma as this his intellect must be trained and disciplined by the severest logical method.

We have seen, then, that the first portion of the *Parmenides* expresses considerable dissatisfaction with the earlier statement of the ideal theory, and at the same time throws out various suggestions with a view to its amendment. Whither all this self-criticism is tending has not yet become clear, but the main results may be summarised as follows. In general, we note a pronounced hesitation in admitting εἴδη αὐτὰ καθ' αὐτὰ of every predicate, coupled with a tendency to distinguish between different classes of εἴδη; secondly, we have an assurance from Parmenides that there will come a time when Socrates will not disdain the lowliest things of nature. In particular, it is shown that the inseparable connexion of ideas with the possibility of predication cannot be reconciled with any view of the nature of the ideas (and we may therefore suppose that Plato henceforward dispenses with that connexion); secondly, that the doctrine of immanence, if understood literally, is inconsistent with the nature of the idea, whether it be transcendentally existent, or a νόημα in the human mind, whereas the expression μίμησις, provided there be no necessity to postulate an idea for every predicate, is perhaps less open to objection; thirdly, that the εἶδος αὐτὸ καθ' αὑτὸ can never be merely a νόημα in the human mind, for a νόημα implies an object, an existent something beyond itself, and this is only the old idea back again; fourthly, that the ideas, although they have been completely severed from the world of time and space, are yet indispensable in the search for truth, since man must always have beyond him a goal on which his eyes may rest. Without some eternal fixity the art of dialectic must perish.

The exact relation borne by the hypotheses of the *Parmenides* to the former half of the dialogue has always been matter of dispute. Ostensibly, of course, they furnish an exercise in logical discipline, and the method employed is similar to the propaedeutic exercise of διάνοια in the *Republic*. That some intimate connexion, however, exists between the subject-matter of the two parts must be the conclusion of all who take Plato seriously. It will be remembered that, at the very beginning of the dialogue, Socrates, relying on the theory of predication that is stated in the *Republic*, joined issue with Zeno, and saw no difficulty in attributing contrary predicates to concrete things, but that on the other hand he did think it impossible that contrary attributes should pertain to the transcendental ideas which informed particulars, and gave them their existence. Such being the state of mind of Socrates at the outset, it would seem reasonable to look for some solution of his original difficulty in the discussion of the eight hypotheses; also, inasmuch as his explanation of contrary predication as connected with ideas has completely broken down, one would expect some light to be thrown on the circumstances of contrary predication. By a brief enumeration of the salient points in the eight hypotheses, I hope to show not only that these expectations are realised, but that considerable progress is made towards the solution of the great dilemma concerning the ideas with which the first part closed.

In the discussion of the first and fourth hypotheses, which stipulate the existence of τὸ ἕν, when ὄν implies self-identity and nothing more, we find it impossible to predicate anything either of τὸ ἕν or of τἆλλα, and where predication is impossible, knowledge is *a fortiori* impossible. On the other hand, from the reasoning of Hypotheses VI and VIII, we conclude that if τὸ ἕν is supposed to be utterly non-existent, it is equally certain that neither predication nor knowledge is possible, whether of ἕν itself or of τἆλλα. If, however, ἕν be conceived of as existing, not merely in self-identity, but in relation to τἆλλα, all manner of predication may take place both in regard to ἕν and to τἆλλα, and knowledge of both ἕν and τἆλλα becomes possible (Hyp. II and III).

Now it is of course obvious that the ἕν of Hypotheses I and IV has an immediate reference to the ἕν of the Eleatic Zeno, and that the inconsistencies arising from his peculiar position are here conspicuously exposed. We are, accordingly, led to infer that τὸ ἕν throughout the hypotheses refers in the first instance to the one supreme reality, whether it be conceived according to the Eleatic or the Platonic scheme. The main result of the six hypotheses mentioned will then be this. The supreme reality, if it is to be known, must have relations with every form of reality, and must have a connexion with all inferior existences. In short, the supreme idea, the ἰδέα τἀγαθοῦ, or whatever else it may be termed, is known only in conjunction with other ideas, and with the infinite flux of sense. Conversely, the flux of sense and the other ideas are to be known only in so far as they are related to the one supreme unity. And if a subordinate idea be for the moment regarded as ἕν, as a unity apart from the supreme idea, it too is to be known only as it enters into combination with the infinite many.

Hypotheses V and VII add to our information concerning this supreme unity. From Hypothesis V we learn that τὸ ἕν may have a negative determination applied to it, and yet be capable of being known, and of bearing descriptive epithets. Here we have of course a foretaste of the justification of τὸ μὴ ὄν in the *Sophist*; it is implied that negative may be as true and as valuable as positive predicates. Hypothesis VII points to a distinction between opinion and knowledge. Assertion of some sort is shown to be possible even where the existence of an all-embracing unity is denied, inasmuch as the plurality of things may be gathered together in aggregates (ὄγκοι), each of which, possessing an apparent unity, enters into apparent relationships with itself and other things. Being mere aggregates, however, they have no organic coherence and fall to pieces when analysed.

Such is the main outcome of the discussion of the

eight hypotheses, but a closer inspection reveals direct
reference to the other problems that are before Plato's
mind. In the first place, αὐτὸ τὸ ἓν at 129 C was
taken as an example of an εἶδος αὐτὸ καθ' αὑτό, and
Socrates there expressed great curiosity to know
whether the idea ἓν could be shown to be πολλά, and
whether in general ideas themselves, in contradistinction to particulars, are capable of diverse predicates,
i.e. of communion with one another. The results of
the hypotheses are an ample proof that such predication
is possible, and that κοινωνία of some sort must exist :
αὐτὸ τὸ ἕν, to be known, must be capable of receiving
all manner of predication, and of entering into all
kinds of relation. But for the final discussion of
this κοινωνία we must look to the later *Sophist* and
Timaeus.

Meantime has any light been thrown on the theory
of predication itself? In a very significant passage at
143 D, E, it is carefully shown that as soon as any
notion, however simple, comes before the mind for
analysis, number is at once generated, and the mind is
forced to count. The notion of number, then, appears
to be a necessity of the mind's action. This principle
applies not only to number, but to all predicates of a
similar kind, as the whole exposition proves. However
slight may be the notion under examination, however
restricted and confined, the mind in passing judgment
is forced to predicate and to make use of a number
of common terms such as like, unlike, same, other,
which express the various relations that one thing
bears to another. Hence, though no dogmatic teaching about predication is to be found, it is taken

for granted from first to last that predication is a *sine qua non* of logical analysis, and that no transcendental explanation need be assumed.

The latter half of the *Parmenides*, then, has made a considerable contribution towards the solution of the problems of the first half. Predication, without which knowledge cannot possibly advance, is shown to be a natural activity of the intellect, and the use of predicates of number, likeness and difference, equality and inequality, etc., is indispensable to the consideration of any subject whatsoever. Moreover, the ideas and the supreme idea, if they are to be not merely existent, but objects of knowledge, must have a real and lasting relation with one another and with the world of sense. Conversely, the world of sense, in so far as it may be known, must be regarded as entering into relation with the supreme unity and its determinations.

Passing on to the *Theaetetus*, we are confronted with another attempt to solve the problem of knowledge. The *Parmenides*, after first demonstrating the impossibility of regarding εἴδη αὐτὰ καθ' αὑτὰ as objects of knowledge, so long as they retain the characteristics ascribed to them in the *Phaedo* and the *Republic*, proceeds to delineate the necessary character of εἴδη if they are to be not merely ὄντα but ἐπιστητά. The *Theaetetus*, falling back on the general question " What is knowledge ?," leads by a process of exhaustion to the same conclusion as the *Parmenides*. Whereas in the *Parmenides* Plato was content to investigate and partially to reconstruct his own view of knowledge, he is now determined to deal no less faithfully with the theories of others, that he may be the more certain of his own system. Hence, in this dialogue and in the *Sophist*, we not only see Socrates endeavouring to test the mental productions of Theaetetus, but Plato himself examining the soundness of his predecessors in philosophy, resolved to discard the dross and retain the gold tried in the furnace of his dialectic.

Theaetetus' first thesis makes ἐπιστήμη identical with αἴσθησις, and in the lengthy conversation that follows we have an estimate of the value attached by Plato to the perpetual flux of sense. By a combination of Protagorean with Heracleitean principles[1] he evolves a theory of sensation by which the fact of sensation depends entirely on the juxtaposition of object and subject; τὸ αἰσθητὸν and τὸ αἰσθανόμενον are each a movement that is generated by the contact. Thus neither the sensation of whiteness nor the colour white has any existence in itself; they are simply the product of the object as ποιοῦν and the subject as πάσχον. As a result, the sensation of whiteness is supposed to reside in the eye, and the colour white is projected outwards by the mind and made to inhere in the object.

This explanation of sensation, which cannot be assigned to any contemporary, and would therefore appear to be that of Plato himself, clearly attributes no permanent reality to the κινήσεις of perceiving or of being perceived: they are γενέσεις that come into being and again depart, varying in character, not only with different subjects, but with the same subject under different circumstances. We conclude, therefore, that

[1] *Theaet.* 182 A, B.

hot and cold, hard and soft, wet and dry, white and black, and the like, have no absolute existence; they count for nothing in the search for reality; they are but the momentary product of the interaction of subject and object. Since they have no existence except in the consciousness of the percipient, and vary indefinitely with different persons, and with the same person at different times, they have no fixed value, and cannot be objects of knowledge. This argument, besides being of supreme weight for the refutation of Theaetetus' first thesis, is of great importance as indicating the tendency of Plato's thought; the character of sensible qualities as secondary products of the activity of mind is maintained throughout the later dialogues, and finds expression in the *Laws*[1]. Moreover, it would be superfluous, in the light of this exposition, to wonder whether Plato still has recourse to an immanent idea to make a particular thing white or hot or sweet, as the language of the *Phaedo* and the *Republic* would indicate. Such qualities now possess neither fixity nor reality; that reality of a kind must appertain to the ποιοῦν and πάσχον which generate them is proved by the later *Sophist*, and marks an important step in Plato's development.

The interest of the argument next centres round Theaetetus' second thesis, viz., ἐπιστήμη is τὸ ὀρθὰ δοξάζειν. Socrates has discovered that the fact of perception is not concerned with sense merely, but that the soul αὐτὴ δι' αὐτῆς compares the data of sensation and passes judgment upon them, assigning or denying to them certain κοινά, or general predicates. These

---

[1] *Laws* 897 A.

16 THE SEARCH FOR KNOWLEDGE

κοινά, ὅμοιον, ἀνόμοιον, ἕν, πλῆθος, etc., carry our
thoughts back to the *Parmenides*, where we had a
practical demonstration of the fact that certain general
predicates are necessary parts of the soul's machinery.
The general aim of this portion of the dialogue, then, is
to show that true opinion, or the process of apprehending
correctly certain κοινά of relation, does not constitute
knowledge. After a long digression on the nature of
false opinion, in which the solution of the *Sophist*,
though not directly stated, is nevertheless implied, and in
which δοξάζειν is shown to apply not merely to sensibles
but to mental abstractions as well, the main thesis is
summarily disposed of by a reference to the rhetorical
art. A man may conceivably pass a true judgment
without having any clear grasp or realisation of the
matter at issue. True opinion may be a factor in
knowledge, but we have not yet seized upon the vital
constituent.

An attempt is immediately made to supply the
deficiency by the addition of a λόγος, i.e., some verbal
expression of the content of true opinion. Various
interpretations of the word λόγος are then mentioned ;
λόγος may mean (*a*) the mere verbal utterance, or
(*b*) the enumeration of elements, in which the Cynics
and Socrates supposed knowledge to consist, or (*c*) the
definition by characteristic difference, Plato's own accep-
tation of the term. Each of these processes in turn is
proved to be insufficient to explain the fact of knowledge ;
they all presuppose the existence of something else
which is known and is the object of knowledge, whereas
they are merely subsidiary to its attainment.

We are, therefore, forced to the conclusion that no

theory of knowledge in which the existence of ideas is not assumed can hope to pass the test of criticism. Mere sensation, as Heracleitean and Protagorean doctrine alike demonstrate, can never furnish a standard. The process of δοξάζειν, or apprehension of relations, may be useful enough, but it is not the sum-total of knowledge. Even the scientific expression of such judgments does not bring us any nearer the goal. Our only hope is to discover as quickly as may be the nature of those εἴδη for which we have long been seeking.

In the *Sophist* there are four subjects that demand our attention—the method of διαίρεσις, the problem of μὴ ὄν, the μέγιστα γένη, and the definition of οὐσία as ἡ τοῦ ποιεῖν ἢ πάσχειν δύναμις. All of these, with the exception of the last, are concerned with the method rather than the object of knowledge, and hence we look to the *Sophist* for enlightenment on the processes of thought and predication rather than for an exposition of the ideas. The method of διαίρεσις, proceeding by subdivision and classification, was first described vaguely in a much earlier dialogue, the *Phaedrus*, and there it was impressed upon us that the essential of good διαίρεσις[1] is to divide κατ' ἄρθρα ᾗ πέφυκε καὶ μὴ ἐπιχειρεῖν καταγνύναι μέρος μηδέν. The same rule is enforced in the διαίρεσις of the *Sophist*, as well as in the similar process in the *Politicus*. The mind, in virtue of its innate power of distinguishing ταὐτόν, θάτερον, ὅμοιον, ἀνόμοιον and the other κοινά, starts from the observation of one common element, and then, proceeding by διαίρεσις κατὰ μέρη, seizes on the characteristic

[1] *Phaedrus* 265 E.

difference of the object to be defined. All definition must be preceded by διαίρεσις, and since definition is the verbal expression of a truth which is known, it follows that διαίρεσις will be an important adjunct to the process of knowledge in general.

The method of διαίρεσις, when applied to the *Sophist*, leads to a consideration of the problem of μὴ ὄν, and finally to the whole question of predication. In the course of a long argument, containing criticisms of the Eleatic and various other schools, it is proved that ὄν and μὴ ὄν may not merely denote Being and Not-Being in the absolute sense, but may signify the positive and negative determinations respectively of the thing to which they are applied. Ὄν, in short, is copulative as well as substantive, and in the former sense both ὄν and μὴ ὄν may be applied to the same thing; μὴ ὄν is simply θάτερον, a category that inheres in all existence.

Closely connected with the subject of μὴ ὄν is the analysis of the five μέγιστα γένη, in which are included the final analysis and solution of the problem of predication, to which there have been continual references in the *Parmenides* and *Theaetetus*. He that would deny the possibility of predication subverts every attempt to form a theory of the universe, and hence the possibility of predication must be accepted as a necessary, axiomatic truth. But, if there is to be predication, we must concede a certain κοινωνία or power of communicability in predicates, since the same thing is capable of receiving various attributes and of entering into various and even contradictory relations. The five great γένη or categories of ὄν,

ταὐτόν, θάτερον, στάσις, κίνησις are then distinguished,
and it is shown that ὄν, ταὐτὸν and θάτερον universally,
and στάσις and κίνησις generally, are found to inhere
together in the same thing, and hence may be said
to have communication one with another.   But although these categories are termed εἴδη and are said
to κοινωνεῖν the one with the other—the requirement
made in the *Parmenides* for the ideal world no less
than the sensible—there is no indication whatever
that ταὐτόν, θάτερον, etc., are the transcendental ideas
which are to be the goal of knowledge; they are
instruments merely which are to aid in the search.
When we come to the *Timaeus*[1], indeed, we find them
definitely classified, not as ideas, but as methods of the
soul's activity.

The conception of falsity, too, is illuminated in the
sections that follow.   Thought, opinion, and imagination are all sometimes false, but this falsity consists
not in the assertion of not-being or nothing, but in
the attribution of things that are not as though they
were.

By far the most significant teaching of the *Sophist*
is to be found at p. 247 E, and the sections that follow.
The materialists, who believe in nothing that they
cannot seize with their hands, are confronted with the
εἰδῶν φίλοι, who place οὐσία and γένεσις at opposite
poles, and deny that there can be any communication
between them.   These latter are, of course, the supporters
of the theory of ideas as originally formulated in the
Phaedo and *Republic*, and Plato, now bent on reconciling
the two conflicting modes of thought, seeks some con-

[1] *Tim.* 35 A seq.

ception of οὐσία which may bridge the gulf that yawns between the ideal and material worlds. Recalling the doctrine of sensation which he had put forward in the *Theaetetus*, he offers a novel definition of οὐσία, viz., ἡ τοῦ ποιεῖν ἢ πάσχειν πρὸς τὸ σμικρότατον δύναμις. Ποιεῖν and πάσχειν are, of course, manifested in various forms, and refer both to the physical activity and passivity of sense, and to the psychical γιγνώσκειν and γιγνώσκεσθαι. It is to be noted, however, that whereas the mind or soul in sensation is πάσχον, in the region of knowledge it is ποιοῦν, and the object of its knowledge, οὐσία, is πάσχον. But the main argument centres in the fact that subject and object are equally in movement, and are therefore equally real forms of οὐσία.

A further step is taken at p. 249. Anything that is ὄντως ὂν must surely, says Plato, possess, not merely movement, but νοῦς, ζωή, and ψυχὴ as well. The statement is, of course, an echo of that theory of soul as being the first and only source of movement which was formulated first in the earlier *Phaedrus*[1] and remained to the end the permanent basis of Plato's philosophy[2]. The important result in the present instance, however, is the inevitable inference that not merely ἡ ψυχὴ ἡ γιγνώσκει, but τὸ γιγνωσκόμενον, whatever it be, is akin to νοῦς and ζωὴ and ψυχή, and must therefore be a form or manifestation of soul. Even the objects of sense, despised though they be because of the Heracleitean flux, may now serve a purpose in the progress of knowledge. Since they too, in some mysterious way, are ποιοῦντα, no less than ψυχή, there must be a reality of some sort underlying them; and we have been assured

[1] *Phaedrus* 245 c.   [2] *Laws* 896 seq.

that the highest reality of all is to be found in the nature of mind and soul.

But though activity, life, soul, mind are inseparable from the ὄντως ὄν, we must be careful, says Plato, not to refuse it also the attributes of permanency and stability. If these were lacking, truly our newly-found reality would be little better than the ῥέοντα of sense, and make us despair once more of attaining to knowledge. Reality, it is true, is possessed of activity and life, but that life and activity are manifested under permanent conditions and according to eternal, immutable modes (κατὰ ταὐτὰ καὶ ὡσαύτως καὶ περὶ τὸ αὐτό). Hence neither motion nor rest is the exclusive attribute of the ὄντως ὄν.

To sum up the results of our investigation, we have, first of all, justified predication on the ground of necessity, and have vindicated the right of the soul to pass judgment on any data supplied to her without the mediation of any exalted and mysterious existences called ideas. Next, in regard to the ideas, it was found at the beginning of the *Parmenides* that so long as the idea possesses the characteristics ascribed to it in the *Phaedo* and *Republic*, knowledge must be forever beyond our reach, and yet that unless the existence of an idea of some sort be assumed, knowledge must remain equally impossible. The *Theaetetus* corroborated this by showing successively that neither sensations, nor those common forms of predication which are essential to the activity of thought, nor yet the scientific expression of thought by definition, connotative or denotative, can in themselves constitute knowledge; they are the instruments, not the objects, of knowledge. We are,

therefore, obliged to postulate ideas, and there is not
wanting a hope that their true nature will finally be
revealed, considerable illumination having already been
gained from the *Parmenides* and the *Sophist*. For the
ideas of the older time are being divided up into classes.
The predicates ὄν and μὴ ὄν, ὅμοιον and ἀνόμοιον, and
the like, are found to be μέγιστα γένη, forms of thought,
essential modes of the soul's activity, and, though they
may retain the old title of εἴδη, they are very different
in kind from the εἴδη αὐτὰ καθ᾽ αὑτὰ of the *Phaedo*,
nor do they carry the significant attributes of the latter.
Sensible qualities, being simply γενέσεις, have no fixity
at all, and cannot assume the importance even of the
μέγιστα γένη. Ethical conceptions of ἀγαθόν, κακόν,
and the like, are in the ordinary way obtained chiefly
through a diligent comparison of past and future[1], and
are relative to circumstance ; on the other hand, there
is a reference to αὐτὴ δικαιοσύνη, αὐτὴ ἀδικία at
Theaetetus 175 C. It is, therefore, uncertain for the
present whether there are still to be ideas of moral
notions or even of natural species, though in regard to
these last we have been told that the meaner things of
nature have an equal claim to respect with the greater.

Under these circumstances it can hardly be denied
that the ideal doctrine of the *Republic*, in which there
was an idea for every predication, did not stand for any
eternal and unassailable truth even in Plato's own mind.
One may almost say, in the words of Jowett[2], that the
earliest ideas were only a " semi-mythical form in which
he attempts to realise abstractions," and they certainly

[1] *Theaet.* 186 A, B.
[2] *Introd. to Cratylus*, p. 623.

were to a large extent "replaced by a rational theory of psychology." Plato, however, is bent on retaining the machinery and terminology of the ideal theory; the assumption of these eternal existences is still indispensable, if he is to explain the universe at all. With the aid of the ideas he kept the Sophists and Cynics at bay while he deliberated about his answer to their most pressing question, viz., "What is Predication?"; and the ideas must still be his stimulus and inspiration if he is yet to satisfy them on the deeper subjects of Knowledge and Being.

For the present, therefore, we are assured that the ideas still exist, though they are fewer in number than heretofore. Furthermore, reality, both as knowing and as known, as acting and as being acted upon, has been declared to be of the nature of mind, and it is in the light of these two general observations that we shall now proceed to interpret the ontology of the dialogues that follow.

ESSAY II.

THE ANALOGY OF THE ARTS AND ITS APPLICATION IN THE *POLITICUS* AND *PHILEBUS*.

A FAVOURITE and effective device of Plato, when intent on the elucidation of ethical and metaphysical truth, is to introduce one or other of the constructive or imitative arts to serve as an illustration. In the earlier dialogues simile and application are alike simple: the statesman is the pilot of the state, the philosopher is the doctor of souls, and so on. But as Plato's powers matured, and his aims grew more ambitious, he began to make a more elaborate and significant use of this instrument. At the beginning of *Republic* X, for instance, the constructive art of the carpenter and the imitative art of the painter serve to illuminate the nature of the ideas, and the kind of relation borne by them to the world of sense. The θεός, who is parallel to the carpenter, makes the ideal bed, which is one and imperishable ; the τέκτων, taking the ideal bed as his παράδειγμα or model, constructs a material bed ; while the painter, with only the material bed as his model, makes an image which is in the third degree removed from ideal truth. The immediate purpose of this, of course, is to degrade mimetic art considerably, and to place it far below constructive art in the scale of truth ; incidentally, however, Plato has shown how valuable an ally the arts may become in the exposition of the ideas. This, coupled with the intimation we had in the *Parmenides* that the ideas might be παραδείγματα ἑστῶτα ἐν τῇ φύσει, and that μίμησις, rather than μέθεξις, should describe the relation borne to them by γιγνόμενα, would reasonably lead us to expect a more extensive use of this metaphor in the dialogues we are now considering. As a matter of fact, Plato in the *Politicus* and the *Philebus* is very largely dependent on constructive art for the adequate expression of his doctrine. In the present paper, therefore, I propose to examine the application of this analogy in these dialogues, hoping that in the sequel some further light may have been thrown on the nature of the ideas, and consequently on the system of knowledge which is the goal of our endeavours.

The first object for our consideration will be a remarkable passage in the *Politicus*, in which Plato gives utterance to his high estimation of an art which has already come prominently forward in the *Protagoras*[1] —the art of measurement. At 283 B, Socrates, in order to show his respondent that their digression on the art of weaving was not too lengthy, declares that the whole nature of excess and defect must be made clear. In the first place, he says, measurement of excess and defect is of two kinds, the first being that which deals with relative size and merely compares one object with another, the other that which judges things according to their approximation to a μέτριον, a

[1] *Protag.* 356 D.

mean, a fixed standard. The latter is by far the
more important; in fact, it is the principle upon which
all γένεσις, all production, is based, and without it the
arts could not exist. Every artist strives to attain a
standard, and in so far as he falls short of this standard,
is his work faulty and bad. Excess and defect are real
evils, and to guard against them is the first necessity
of art.

Now it is plain that the usual connotation of μέτριον
and of μετρητική has been considerably extended in
this exposition. At the outset, τὸ μέτριον would seem
to signify a unit or norm of measurement, in reference
to which things relatively great or small may be
accurately measured. But this simple meaning is soon
superseded, for at 284 A seq. we learn that the arts
make use of τὸ μέτριον, not as a norm or unit of
measurement, but as an ideal, a standard, by the
attainment of which alone things ἀγαθὰ and καλὰ are
produced. Hence μετρητική, in this new Platonic
sense, is not merely an art of measurement, but an art
which compares the productions of τέχνη[1] with τὸ
πρέπον καὶ τὸ δέον. It is a critical science, which
passes judgment on σκευαστὰ in virtue of a fixed
standard, with which it is acquainted. At the same
time it is to be noticed that the connexion of μετρητική
with spatial and mathematical measure is apparently
maintained throughout, inasmuch as it is described at
the final summing-up[2] as including ὁπόσαι τέχναι τὸν
ἀριθμὸν καὶ μήκη καὶ βάθη καὶ πλάτη πρὸς τὸ μέτριον
καὶ τὸ πρέπον καὶ τὸν καιρὸν μετροῦσι. In short, τὸ
μέτριον, in relation to the arts, is an ideal standard,

―――――――――――――――
[1] 284 E.   [2] 284 E.

consisting of certain fixed mathematical combinations, or proportions, to which the products of the arts should approximate.

Such being clearly the significance of τὸ μέτριον in the arts, our next step will be to determine its value when employed in the demonstration of metaphysical truth. At 284 D Socrates expresses his conviction that, at some future time, this notion of τὸ μέτριον will be called into requisition πρὸς τὴν περὶ αὐτὸ τἀκριβὲς ἀπόδειξιν. We therefore expect to hear more of it, and our expectation is fully realised in the *Philebus*.

At 16 B, C, of the *Philebus* there occurs a remarkable reference to the process of διαίρεσις, of which Socrates remarks[1], ἧς ἐγὼ ἐραστής εἰμι ἀεί. This method has been responsible for every great discovery of the arts, and it is based on the principle that ἕν and πολλὰ are to be found everywhere, and that πέρας and ἄπειρον, limit and infinity, are inherent in the very nature of things. It is, therefore, the duty of the dialectician to posit one εἶδος for every infinity of particulars, and not to rest satisfied until he has discovered the definite number (ὁπόσα) of species that are to be inserted between.

This general reference to πέρας and ἄπειρον, as representing in the abstract that which can be accurately estimated and defined, as contrasted with that which defies determination and classification, prepares us for the more abstruse discussion of these notions at 23 C seq. At this point of the dialogue Socrates has proved that τὸ ἀνθρώπινον ἀγαθόν (the discovery of which is the sole aim of the treatise), is to be identified

---

[1] Cf. *Phaedrus* 266 B.

with neither of the two claimants, νοῦς and ἡδονή, in separation, but that it must consist in a μικτὸς βίος, which is the compound of both. It is at the same time maintained by Socrates that the ingredient in this μικτὸς βίος which makes it ἀγαθὸν is more akin to νοῦς than to ἡδονή, and that, if this can be proved, the life of reason must be awarded the second prize. With a view to demonstrating this superiority of νοῦς over ἡδονή, he proposes to examine both, and to place them, according to their merits, in one or other of four classes, within which, he says, πάντα τὰ νῦν ὄντα ἐν τῷ παντὶ are contained.

Now the classification here referred to, in which the notions of πέρας and ἄπειρον reappear, is primarily a dissection, as it were, of the universe based on metaphysical principles. Such is the immediate inference one draws from the impressive manner in which the subject is introduced (τὸν θεὸν ἐλέγομέν που τὸ μὲν ἄπειρον δεῖξαι τῶν ὄντων, τὸ δὲ πέρας), and from the fact that the first intimation of the division into ἄπειρον and πέρας[1] came as a suggestion regarding the solution of those inconsistencies which marred the theory of ideas. Moreover, the divisions themselves accord most easily with this interpretation. It is not the first time that the notions ἄπειρον and πέρας have been conjoined in a metaphysical analysis of reality. In the second and third hypotheses of the *Parmenides*, where a similar classification is evolved, there is an undoubted reference to metaphysical theory[2]. There we find ἐν representing the supreme ideal unity, and τἆλλα the world of phenomena, also the adjectives πεπερασμένα

[1] 15 A, B.   [2] *Parm.* 144 E; 158 D.

and ἄπειρα applied as essential characteristics to τἆλλα. These four correspond in inverse order to the ἄπειρον, πέρας, μικτὸν and αἰτία of the *Philebus*. Our conclusion is reinforced again by the fact that the fourth and greatest class, the αἰτία τῆς μίξεως, is proclaimed to be νοῦς, which governs both universe and individual, since our examination of the *Sophist*[1] has proved indisputably that νοῦς is henceforward to have the pre-eminence in Plato's explanation of the universe.

Since the classification then appears to rest on a metaphysical basis, one would expect to find the metaphysical principle faithfully adhered to throughout. Plato's avowed object in this dialogue, however, is not metaphysical but practical; he wishes to arrive at a logical determination of the ἀνθρώπινον ἀγαθόν. Hence the metaphysical classification throughout the argument is made subservient to practical considerations, and it is apparently appropriated simply in order that some unique authority, as it were, may support Socrates in his estimate of the three different lives. This peculiarity, combined with the generally confused and ` fragmentary state of the dialogue, makes it extremely difficult to arrive with certainty at the original significance of the four γένη. The μικτὸν γένος, which should properly include only the unions of metaphysical ἄπειρα and πέρατα, is made to contain the μικτὸς βίος, a union of an ἄπειρον, ἡδονή, not with πέρας, but with an αἰτία (νοῦς); ἡδονή[2], too, is classed at one time under τὸ ἄπειρον, at another under τὸ μικτόν; and at 26 A, B, ὥρα, which, in so far as it denotes a certain atmospheric state, is surely to be ranked with χειμὼν and πνῖγος in

---

[1] *Soph.* 249 A seq.   [2] 27 E; 31 A, B, C.

a table of metaphysical valuations, is separated from them on the fanciful ground that good things cannot be classed with ἄπειρα, which are evil. It is clear that the same principle of classification is not maintained throughout. Plato has, in fact, for the purposes of the dialogue, turned a set of metaphysical distinctions into a loose, popular classification; and, since our aim is to arrive at his metaphysical teaching, we must endeavour to describe the four γένη as they appear when divested of those inconsistencies which are peculiar to the dialogue.

It must, first of all, be noted that the whole classification here is based upon the analogy of the constructive arts. The universe is regarded as a living κόσμος, a whole compounded of body and soul, and containing within it all inferior bodies and souls. Within this κόσμος is going on continually a process of μῖξις or γένεσις (the very word used for artistic production in the *Politicus*), and all the four kinds of ὄντα of which τὸ πᾶν consists are, in one capacity or another, involved in this γένεσις. Now it was shown in the *Politicus* that the first essential of every art is a μέτριον, or ideal standard, in accordance with which the particular product is fashioned. Besides this, however, we know that there is needed first, ὕλη, or τὸ πρωτογενὲς κτῆμα of *Politicus* 288 E, ἐξ ὧν καὶ ἐν οἷς δημιουργοῦσιν ὁπόσαι τῶν τεχνῶν νῦν εἴρηνται; secondly, the ὄργανα συναίτια of *Politicus* 287 D; and thirdly, the artist or δημιουργὸς himself. Of these τὸ μέτριον undoubtedly corresponds to πέρας in the *Philebus*, inasmuch as it is definitely identified with it at 24 C and 66 A, and is moreover described as being

the cause of μετριότης and συμμετρία¹ in its μικτά.
The artist's ὕλη is to be correlated with the ἄπειρον,
into which τὸ πέρας is said to enter, thereby producing
a μικτὸν compounded of both². The whole language
of the passage implies that πέρας is applied to ἄπειρον
as form to material. That the αἰτία is parallel to the
δημιουργὸς follows obviously from its description³ as τὸ
ποιοῦν and τὸ πάντα τὰ γιγνόμενα δημιουργοῦν. As
to the ὄργανα συναίτια, some doubt may at present
exist as to their identification, but we cannot go far
wrong in connecting them, provisionally at least, with
the πέρας, which, in company with τὸ ἄπειρον, is called
τὸ δουλεῦον εἰς γένεσιν αἰτίᾳ⁴. A more complete analysis of all these conceptions must now be attempted.

Beginning then with the class of ὕλη, what is the
essential nature of τὸ ἄπειρον, and what things are
included in it ? Socrates tells us that it is the class of
τὸ μᾶλλον καὶ ἧττον, and that the quality of indefiniteness is inherent in it. Its nature is such as to forbid
any application of τέλος or ποσόν; as soon as any such
notion is connected with it, it loses its characteristic
and ceases to be what it is (αὐτὼ τετελευτήκατον).
The class is made up of θερμότερον καὶ ψυχρότερον,
ξηρότερον καὶ ὑγρότερον, πλέον καὶ ἔλαττον, θᾶττον
καὶ βραδύτερον, μεῖζον καὶ σμικρότερον, and the like,
of everything, in fact, that admits of τὸ σφόδρα καὶ τὸ
ἠρέμα. Τὸ ἡδὺ καὶ τὸ λυπηρόν, therefore, would come
under the same category⁵—a fact which is explicitly
acknowledged by Socrates quite apart from any reference
to the quantitative hedonism of Philebus. At 31 B, it is

¹ 64 E ; 65.   ² 24 C, D.   ³ 26 E ; 27 B.   ⁴ 27 A.
⁵ 28 A ; 31 A ; 41 D.

true, there is a temporary lapse of consistency, and he speaks of it as a μικτόν, but there, as in other places, the metaphysical interest has been superseded, and Socrates is looking at pleasure and pain as concrete facts, and is seeking to define them on a popular basis.

Now this talk of hotter and colder, drier and wetter, with the accompanying statement of their indefiniteness and of the impossibility of applying to them any fixed character, takes our minds back to the earlier part of the *Theaetetus*, where all the qualities dependent on sensation came in for a vigorous examination. As a result, we found that all these qualities, being due to a κίνησις between subject and object, had no existence except in the consciousness of the percipient. They were subjective phenomena, varying indefinitely with different subjects and therefore possessing no fixed value. Their apparent externality, too, was due to the percipient subject alone, which projected outside itself a something[1] which could not have come into being apart from itself. Τὸ ἄπειρον, then, is the class of hotter and colder, of subjective affections, which vary indefinitely and have no claim on real existence. The comparative form in which they are expressed serves to stamp them with the mark of unceasing variableness, and one feels inclined, with Natorp[2], to see in them a striking resemblance to the ὄγκοι of the *Parmenides*[3], which bear relation to one another only, and of which the least part, as well as the greatest, is branded as infinity.

Sensible qualities, then, in general, serve as ὕλη in

[1] *Theaet.* 156 E seq.
[2] Natorp, *Plato's Ideenlehre* (Leipzig 1903).
[3] *Parm.* 164, 165.

the production of the μικτὰ of the universe. But
there are not wanting certain signs which show that
a far more subtle conception is, at any rate, at the back
of Plato's mind, even though it may not as yet have
taken definite shape. At 24 D we hear of ἡ τοῦ μᾶλλον
καὶ ἧττον ἕδρα, into which τὸ ποσὸν and τὸ μέτριον
are supposed to enter, and which evidently is that
which affords a place, a home, for these ἄπειρα, such
as they are. Now it is, of course, impossible to conceive of anything as subject to infinite fluctuation, like
the ἄπειρα, without at the same time allowing to
it extension of some kind, in which the fluctuations
may take place; we should remember, moreover, that
τὸ μεῖζον καὶ σμικρότερον[1] is one of the ἄπειρα, and the
ἕδρα of an ἄπειρον of this sort would be very definitely
extension, and nothing else. Hence the ἕδρα must
inevitably be identified with extension, the home of
fluctuation and Becoming, although the slight use
made of it at this juncture forbids us to lay any great
stress on the conception at present. The final analysis
of extension does not concern Plato in the *Philebus*,
and he may or may not have intended to make it the
πέμπτον γένος which is mentioned so casually at 23 D.

The ὕλη, then, of the world-process is in the
Philebus made to consist of sensible qualities, with
a slight but unmistakeable reference to a ἕδρα, in
which the qualities reside, and which is the inevitable
condition of the γένεσις of the μικτά. In fact, there
would seem to be here a distinct use of the two functions
of ὕλη which are mentioned at *Politicus* 288 D (ἐξ ὧν
καὶ ἐν οἷς δημιουργοῦσιν αἱ τέχναι).

[1] 25 C.

We now come to the class of πέρας, and here
a difficulty awaits us, although it would at first sight
seem quite easy to identify it with τὸ μέτριον of the
Politicus. Here, as elsewhere in the dialogue, Plato
does not seem to have one clear conception in mind
throughout. The class as a whole is styled τὸ πέρας,
or the limit. But as early as 24 c we hear of two
sorts of πέρας, called respectively τὸ ποσὸν and τὸ
μέτριον, the very names of which indicate a difference
in kind. Our knowledge of the *Politicus* naturally
makes us think of τὸ μέτριον as an ideal standard,
dependent indeed upon mathematical determinations,
but only in the sense that a law is dependent upon the
material in which it finds expression. That the same
signification attaches to it here would seem to follow
from its equation with τὸ καίριον and ἡ ἀΐδιος φύσις
at 66 A. As for ποσόν, it would appear to signify
quantity, or magnitude, and nothing further.

This distinction within τὸ πέρας is immediately borne
out by the special mention[1] of τὸ πέρας ἔχον, that which
contains or possesses limit, and ἡ τοῦ πέρατος γέννα[2], the
offspring of limit, which are evidently identical with
each other and with τὸ ποσόν. The examples which
Plato cites, τὸ ἴσον, τὸ διπλάσιον, καὶ πᾶν ὅ τί περ ἂν
πρὸς ἀριθμὸν ἀριθμὸς ἢ μέτρον ἢ πρὸς μέτρον, are all
mathematical determinations, just the relations that
are essential to the expression of a mathematical
proportion or law, such as the μέτριον of the *Politicus*
was found to be.

We cannot, therefore, go far wrong in dividing τὸ
πέρας into two classes, τὸ μέτριον and τὸ ποσόν, the first

[1] 24 A.   [2] 25 D.

representing the ideal law which governs the production of μικτά, the second the mathematical magnitudes and relations through which it works. This conclusion finds special confirmation in the language of a succeeding passage, for at 26 D the whole process of μῖξις is described as a "generation into existence out of numerical relations established with the agency of limit" (γένεσις εἰς οὐσίαν ἐκ τῶν μετὰ τοῦ πέρατος ἀπειργασμένων μέτρων). The μέτριον of the artist, then, is parallel to the μέτριον that governs the γένεσις of the universe, and which is an immaterial law, finding best expression in a later sentence of the dialogue [1]: κόσμος τις ἀσώματος ἄρξων καλῶς ἐμψύχου σώματος; and the ὄργανα συναίτια are surely nothing else than the ποσά, the πέρατος γέννα, which are the indispensable instruments through which the μέτριον operates.

The class of μικτὰ should not detain us long, for they are a multitude in number [2], and the most easily identified of all. They cover the whole realm of concrete existence, and include every discoverable species of the natural world. Unfortunately, however, Plato has here signally failed in clearness of thought and language, and at this juncture of the argument he seems to be governed entirely by the practical considerations of the dialogue, leaving out of sight the metaphysical principle on which the division is primarily based. Since the μικτὸς βίος, upon which the whole argument bears, is not a natural μικτόν, but an imaginary conception, it is only μικτὰ of this kind that he chooses to cite as examples, things which are μικτά, not in a meta-physical, but in a figurative, sense. Acting thus on

[1] 64 B.　　　　　　　　[2] 26 c.

the popular belief that all evil is ἄπειρον, all good πεπερασμένον, he mentions ὑγίεια, κάλλος and ἰσχὺς as typical members of the mixed class; whereas the whole trend of the argument is to show that these words signify, not μικτὰ themselves, but attributes which attach to them when they are faithful copies of τὸ μέτριον. They are the scientific terms applied by the mind in its capacity of critic, and are therefore to be classed with νοῦς as a part of its machinery. As for μουσική, it is obviously out of place among the μικτὰ here. Μουσικὴ is a constructive art, and it is constructive art that supplies the analogy upon which this whole classification of the physical universe is based; nothing could be more unreasonable than to introduce a simile as part of its application. We are satisfied, therefore, that μικτά, in strictness, represent natural substances and nothing more.

With regard to the αἰτία, which corresponds to the δημιουργὸς of the arts, we are told in indisputable language [1] that it is νοῦς and nothing else. But what aspect of νοῦς? At this crisis of the argument Socrates declares in most impressive language that the universe, so far from being ruled by blind force, is controlled by a universal νοῦς and σοφία, and that this universal νοῦς is the source of our inferior intelligences, just as surely as our bodies are derived from its body. Clearly then the cause of the universe is inseparably connected with the universal νοῦς, but not, I may remark, with the universal νοῦς regarded as separate from the universe; the νοῦς of 30 A seq. is not only present in all things, but is distributed especially into the finite

[1] *Phil.* 30 c.

souls of men. The ἀνθρώπινος νοῦς is bound up with the universal νοῦς, and shares with it the function of αἰτία, just as in the *Sophist*[1] divine and human νοῦς alike are centres of activity.

In other passages, of course, where the αἰτία τῆς μίξεως is not in question, we find the divine νοῦς regarded as something apart from the universe, as pure intellectual activity[2], that which represents the most divine life of all. But this ἀληθινὸς καὶ θεῖος νοῦς suffers neither pleasure nor pain, and is liable to none of those affections which limit the capacities of men. Its entire separation from the influences of body raises it above all participation in the physical universe. The divine reason in this aspect, therefore, cannot be the universal νοῦς distributing itself into finite intelligences, nor can it be regarded as mingling ἄπειρα (subjective phenomena) with ποσά (mathematical relations peculiar to the human intellect) in order to produce material things. The θεῖος νοῦς, considered as pure intellect in continual activity, is single and separate; but, in its character of αἰτία τῆς μίξεως, it must be regarded as multiform, and as acting through the subordinate intelligences of which it is the source.

Our analysis of Plato's four γένη thus results in a view of the universe, and of the material things of which it is composed, as a generation and as a mixture of certain ingredients brought about by a definite agent. Material things are compounds of sensible qualities and mathematical determinations, fused together by the universal νοῦς, regarded as acting plurally through the inferior minds into which it is subdivided, and

[1] *Soph.* 248 E.   [2] 22 C.

as copying an immaterial ideal law which expresses itself in the mathematical relations aforesaid. Here truly is an explanation of phenomenal existence which in subtlety and power far transcends the older theory, in which we were told, indeed, of an infinite world of ideas, but which threw no light whatever on the function or *modus operandi* of those ideas.

Some doubt has existed as to whether the doctrine of the *Philebus* admits of ideas at all, and the four γένη have been regarded as a by-product of Plato's thought. A careful consideration of the class of πέρας, however, combined with the knowledge that the imperative necessity of revising the ideal theory [1] was in Plato's mind as he wrote, leads us to the conclusion that in the πέρας he had at last arrived at a conception of the ideas which his critics were powerless to assail. To this it has been frequently objected that the difficulty of 15 B, viz., that the idea exists both apart from, and immanent in, particulars, is not thereby removed. Such an objection, however, does not appear to take account of the division of τὸ πέρας into τὸ μέτριον and τὸ ποσόν, of which τὸ μέτριον alone represents the idea, τὸ ποσὸν the instrument of its operation. Transcendence and immanence are still its characteristics, but the new explanation of its nature practically reconciles the two. The law of proportion which governs the production of a μικτὸν is certainly something other than the μικτὸν itself, removed from it as far as the ideal is removed from the material, but it is also in a sense immanent in the μικτόν, since it gives to the latter its characteristics, and is itself

[1] 15 B.

illustrated therein in virtue of its representatives, the ποσά. Such then is the character of the idea as portrayed in the *Philebus*; it is a law of mathematical proportion which governs the generation of phenomenal things, that is, not *merely* a scientific generalisation attained through observation and experiment, but rather an eternal necessity inherent in the very nature of a thing and expressing its peculiar reality. Further light on this notion, however, must be reserved till we come to the examination of the *Timaeus*.

An important question remains. Of what things are there ideas of this sort, and where is the line to be drawn? To this the exposition of the γένη seems to provide a clear answer. There are ideas of all μικτά, and the μικτά of the material universe are surely every species of natural substance, whether animate or inanimate, organic or inorganic. The mere fact that sensible qualities, mathematical relations, mind and all its activities in art and science, are to be found *outside* the class of μέτριον serves to rule them out of the list of ideas; and of these the first two classes were already, in the *Theaetetus*, *Parmenides*, and *Sophist*, banished from the realm of the ideas.

A few words should be said in regard to two classes of existences which are not included in those mentioned above. The first of these, σκευαστά, of which, like everything else, there were ideas [1] in the time of the *Republic*, seems since then to have declined in importance. In the critique of the *Parmenides* [2] Socrates apparently does not think it worth while even to mention them, and the same applies to *Philebus* 15 A. They have, it

[1] See *Crat.* 389 A.   [2] *Parm.* 130 c.

is true, served a purpose, and no slight one, in affording
a striking analogy, which Plato has used with effect in
both the *Philebus* and the *Timaeus*, for the elucidation of
the ideal doctrine. It is, however, quite incredible
that Plato should have included them in the μικτά of
the universe, which are subject to the μέτριον imposed
by universal νοῦς. If they are to be placed in the
γένη at all, it must be as an appendage to the class of
νοῦς, which, as we gather from 66 B, includes ἐπιστῆμαι
and τέχναι of all sorts, and, presumably, their products
also.

The other class of existences referred to, that of τὸ
ὑγιεινόν, τὸ ἀγαθόν, τὸ καλόν, etc., is of far greater
importance, and certainly of greater philosophical
significance, since they have served as typical examples
of ideal reality from the time of the *Symposium* onwards[1].
They are not, however, natural μικτά, and, consequently,
it is impossible, from the point of view of the *Philebus*,
to attribute to them a μέτριον in the same sense in
which it applies to the others. In order to determine
their essential nature, we must examine for a moment
the conception of Good as revealed at the close of the
dialogue. At 64 A there is thrown out a hint to the
effect that by an analysis of a special μικτόν, viz., the
μικτὸς βίος, we may hope to learn τί ποτε ἔν τε ἀνθρώπῳ
καὶ τῷ παντὶ πέφυκεν ἀγαθὸν καὶ τίνα ἰδέαν αὐτὴν
εἶναί ποτε μαντευτέον. Then follow immediately the
three criteria by which a thing is judged to be good
or the reverse. These criteria, in contradistinction to
the popular requirements of τέλειον, ἱκανόν, αἱρετόν,
have a metaphysical bearing, and are, first of all,

[1] Cf. *Theaet.* 175 c; *Phil.* 15 A; 62 A.

ἀλήθεια, secondly, μετριότης, and thirdly, συμμετρία. Now it is obvious from the confused arrangement of the passage that these three notions are employed loosely, and that they are in reality closely akin to one another, being different aspects of the same thing. 'Αλήθεια, in Plato's strict usage, always implies correspondence with an ideal reality, and that this is its application here seems to follow from the fact that the principle of valuation is no longer popular, but metaphysical. Μετριότης, if we are to keep to the new sense of μέτριον established in the *Politicus* and the *Philebus*, will mean the quality of being μέτριον, or of conforming to τὸ μέτριον, i.e., the ideal standard; whereas συμμετρία, the condition of a whole when its parts are duly proportioned, will represent the material aspect of μετριότης[1], since it is conformity with the μέτριον that makes the particular ingredients perceptibly symmetrical. It is, accordingly, clear that there is in reality only one criterion of the good. The most general term for it is ἀλήθεια, which signifies approximation to the ideal. The expression most characteristic of the *Philebus* is μετριότης, since it implies the special interpretation of the ideal which the *Philebus* presents. Finally, μετριότης reveals itself in the concrete particular as συμμετρία, or harmonious relation of parts, and is, in this aspect, the cause of κάλλος. The test of goodness, then, in the material universe at least, is approximation to the μέτριον, and this test, says Plato, holds *whatever* be the μικτὸν under consideration. Hence τὸ ἀγαθὸν and τὸ κάλλος, when applied to the μικτὰ of the universe, are no longer suprasensual realities; they are rather part of the machinery of a

[1] See 25 E.

particular science, a science of μετρητική, whose function it is to compare things, not with one another, but
with the absolute μέτριον which is the law of their
existence. In the *Politicus* we became acquainted
with a science of art-criticism, which looked upon all
divergence from the standard as an evil, which must in
all cases be avoided; and now we find that there is a
still higher μετρητική, a science of ideal aesthetics,
whose business it is to judge the γιγνόμενα of the world
in the light of the absolute idea. But the Good and
the Beautiful are not ideas, which inhere in μικτά, and
thereby make them materially good and beautiful;
they are simply terms of relation, a part of the
machinery which every art must have, and they are to
be ranked, not with the ideas, but with the τέχναι,
which are an appendage to νοῦς. In the region of
ethics, indeed, we have yet to show that Plato was to
the end faithful to his belief in a supreme αὐτὸ ἀγαθὸν
or its equivalent: in the *Timaeus* we are presented
with his final standard of moral goodness. But, in
everything that concerns the physical excellence of
γιγνόμενα, he is now content to point to the μέτριον of
each thing as the supreme test of its value.

We have, therefore, in succession excluded from
the ideal world sensible qualities, relations, objects of
ἐπιστῆμαι and τέχναι, σκευαστά, and also the terms
good and beautiful and their opposites; and the word
εἶδος or ἰδέα is henceforward to be applied especially
to the organic types of nature, and all species of natural
substances.

But what steps must be taken in order to discover
these μέτρια? If Plato means them to take the place
of the old ἰδέαι as objects of knowledge, how are they

to become known to us? Surely in the way which Plato himself has indicated. At a very early stage[1] of the dialogue Socrates brings up the eternal question of the One and the Many, and Protarchus, with youthful ardour, is anxious to attack it then and there in its most subtle form, viz., in its application to the theory of ideas. The only way, says Socrates, to unravel the mystery of the One and the Many in any form is to make use of the old method of διαίρεσις, which he had employed many a time in his search for truth, in the region of politics and ethics no less than in metaphysics. Limit and unlimitedness are present everywhere, not only in the physical universe, but in the realm of knowledge too : the very method of definition is founded on a recognition of the two principles. Whatever then it be that we seek to know, let us posit one genus for it, and then in the light of this genus resolve the indefinity of the individual representatives into a definite number of species, among which the object of our search will be found. The true nature of μέτρια is accordingly to be discovered by the use of this supremely efficient instrument; careful analysis of the indefinity of particulars will reveal the nature of the species, as well as of the genus. The μέτριον of either is the eternal law of proportion which governs it, and it cannot but reveal itself to him who makes search with diligence. Of so much we are for the present assured : but for a comprehensive view of the whole scheme of knowledge and of its detailed dependence upon the theory of ideal Being, we must look to the *Timaeus*, which now awaits our consideration.

[1] 14 c seq.

ESSAY III.

THE WORLD-PROCESS OF THE *TIMAEUS*.

In our consideration of the *Philebus* we were called
upon to regard the world as the result of a process or
generation analogous to that which is concerned with
production in the arts. The universe, we were told, is
a γιγνόμενον, a product brought into being by the
agency of νοῦς, which combines sensible qualities with
mathematical relations, and makes them conform to
certain μέτρια, or eternal laws of formation. In the
myth of the *Timaeus* we find this doctrine not merely
reiterated, but extended and developed in the greatest
detail, and with a far more elaborate use of the symbol-
ism with which we are already acquainted. The whole
cosmos, with all its various interrelated parts, in all its
activities both great and small, is spread out before us
in one of the most magnificent allegories that the world
has ever seen. Abstract conceptions, which in the
Sophist were presented to us in logical simplicity, are
here displayed in the picturesque dress of personifica-
tion ; the universe is represented as being constructed
after a material fashion out of the immaterial elements
into which Plato has analysed it in thought. Our
present object is to make a general estimate of the
purport of the myth, reserving for separate treatment

its bearing upon Plato's final statement regarding the nature of knowledge.

A brief *résumé* of the story till the end of c. xvi[1], which marks a definite break in the exposition, is the first essential. First of all, says Plato, it behoves us to draw a distinction between that which is and that which becomes, between τὸ ὂν ἀεί, γένεσιν δ᾽ οὐκ ἔχον, and τὸ γιγνόμενον μὲν ἀεί, ὂν δὲ οὐδέποτε : the first is apprehended by reason alone, the second is the object of opinion and irrational sensation. To which of these does the universe belong ? Surely, since it is visible and tangible, and generally apprehensible by δόξα and αἴσθησις, to that which is γιγνόμενον and not ὄν. But the peculiarity of the phenomenal is that it always has an αἰτία, hence one must be found for the universe. Moreover, a thing can only be fair when the δημιουργὸς who fashions it takes the ideal as his model ; that the universe is fair no one can dispute ; it is κάλλιστος τῶν γεγονότων. Therefore, whatever be its cause, the ideal must be the model upon which it is built.

Now, in order that the universe might be καλόν, its αἰτία, or, to adopt the language of " production," artificer produced in it harmony and measure, and also, seeing that of sensible things that which possesses νοῦς is always superior to that which has it not, he placed νοῦς in ψυχὴ and ψυχὴ in σῶμα, since apart from ψυχὴ νοῦς cannot inhere in anything. As for the παράδειγμα, in imitation of which the world was fashioned, it is a ζῷον, the all-embracing νοητὸν ζῷον, containing in itself all other νοητὰ ζῷα, τὸ κάλλιστον τῶν νοουμένων.

[1] *Tim.* 47 E.

As for the σῶμα of the cosmos, it is composed of the whole sum of fire, air, earth and water. These four ingredients are essential, since, although two only, fire and earth, are requisite for visibility and tangibility, two others must be added as means in order to make the resultant body a perfect unity. This body is a perfect whole made up of perfect parts; and, seeing that it includes within itself all animals, it possesses that shape which comprehends all other shapes, viz., the spherical. It has no need of organs, but revolves upon its own axis in a uniform circular motion, the motion most typical of the action of νοῦς and φρό-νησις.

But, although we have spoken of ψυχὴ as being placed within body, we do not therefore imply that σῶμα is older or of greater importance than ψυχὴ which inheres in it. The truth is rather to be expressed in this way : ψυχὴ rules over σῶμα, and penetrates it through and through. It is composed of three ingre-dients ; the ἀμέριστος and ἀεὶ κατὰ ταὐτὰ ἔχουσα οὐσία, and that which, being divided in material bodies, is γιγνόμενον, ὂν δὲ οὐδέποτε, are mingled with a third form of οὐσία which is, like them, compounded of ταὐτὸν and θάτερον[1]. These three forms of οὐσία the artificer welded together into a unity, hard though it was to mingle θάτερον with ταὐτόν. Further, he divided the mixture thus formed into portions corre-sponding to the intervals of the diatonic scale ; after which, the whole of soul being divided into two halves,

[1] This rendering of the sentence beginning τῆς ἀμερίστου (35 A) has the authority, among ancient commentators, of Proclos and Plutarch (περὶ τῆς ἐν Τιμαίῳ ψυχογονίας, c. 25).

he laid them across one another in the shape of the letter X, and formed of them two intersecting circles. The one of these, which revolved to the right by way of the side, he called the circle of ταὐτόν, that which revolved to the left diagonally, the circle of θάτερον. To the circle of ταὐτὸν he not only gave supremacy over the circle of θάτερον, but he left it single and undivided, whereas the circle of θάτερον was cleft into seven concentric circles corresponding to the orbits of the seven planets.

Next, in order to make the κόσμος resemble still more its eternal παράδειγμα, he produced within it an everlasting image of eternity, which has been named time, and for the measurement of which he fashioned the planets which revolve in the seven orbits of θάτερον. All these, together with the fixed stars, are living deities, spherical in shape, composed chiefly of fire, but whereas the fixed stars follow the motion of the Same only, which is most like to the activity of reason, the planets are endowed with the motions of Same and Other both.

The universe, however, was not yet complete, for as many varieties of ἰδέαι as νοῦς beholds in the αὐτὸ ζῷον, so many the artificer thought should be contained in the ὁρατὸν ζῷον ; and of these there are, besides the θεῖον γένος of stars, three inferior classes, viz., the tribes which inhabit the air, the water, and the earth. With a view to the making of these, he called together the race of heavenly stars, and, addressing them as θεοὶ θεῶν, showed how τὸ πᾶν could not be truly πᾶν until there were placed within it the inferior animals also ; yet he himself could not make these, for they would

thus become the equal of the deities themselves, whose
bodies had been rendered indissoluble by his own will.
Consequently to the stars he assigned the duty of
moulding for the νοητὰ ζῶα such bodies as were
appropriate for them, as well as the task of providing
them with sustenance, and of receiving them again at
death. But, before he committed to the deities the
immortal principle of the ζῶα, he took such portion of
the three ingredients as was left over from the former
mixture, and, having compounded it in less perfect
proportions, he divided the whole into individual souls
equal in number to the fixed stars. These souls, being
placed each in one of the stars as in a chariot, were
then shown the nature of the universe and its inevitable
laws : how that they should each be planted in one of
the planets, and that it was given to them to choose
how they would live ; if they lived in righteousness,
they should hereafter return to their kindred star and
be happy, but if otherwise, they must pass in graduated
stages first into the form of a woman, and thereafter
into the forms of beasts in due order, according to their
manner of life. Then the planetary gods, obeying the
command of their father, made mortal bodies of the
four elements they found in the universe, and these
bodies they made so far as possible in the image of
the cosmic and starry bodies, placing the circles of
ταὐτὸν and θάτερον within the spherical body called
the head. At birth the soul of the creatures thus
made was overcome with disorder and tumult, owing to
the disturbances caused by the influx of nourishment
and the impact of external sensations. The circle of
the Same was impeded and the circle of the Other

distorted, so that neither Reason nor Sensation func-
tioned correctly. In time, however, the commotion
abated and the motions of the Same and Other resumed
their proper course ; then might such a soul, if it used
its opportunities aright, attain to the excellence of
knowledge and intellectual liberty.

All the rest of the body, hands, feet, and sense-
organs, were given merely to minister to the comfort
of the head, which was its divinest part. Sight and
hearing, and all our senses, were bestowed for this one
purpose, that, through observing the orbits of heavenly
beings, we might be enabled to order aright the
revolution of reason in our own souls, and pursue divine
philosophy, the greatest gift of God to men.

So much will suffice for an examination of the main
principles of the myth ; the detailed physical exposition
that follows may well claim our attention in a separate
paper. First of all a word or two must be said as to
the claims of this story to be considered as an allegory
at all. Such a view of it is assuredly no novelty, for it
apparently prevailed in the Platonic school from the
time of Aristotle onwards. The latter refers distinctly
to such an interpretation in *de Caelo*[1] ; Plutarch, too,
though maintaining a literal interpretation himself[2], is
obviously conscious that the opposite view was the
favourite among his contemporaries. Aristotle, in *de
Caelo*, pours contempt upon those who compare the
simile of creation in time to a diagram, in explanation
of which tense-forms are used, not to indicate time-
relation, but merely with a view to clearness in expo-

[1] Ar. *de Caelo* i. 10.
[2] Plutarch, περὶ τῆς ἐν Τιμαίῳ ψυχογονίας.

W.   4

sition. The cases, he says, are not parallel, for all the separate parts of a diagram can co-exist, whereas ἀταξία and τάξις, which in the *Timaeus* are made to follow one another, can never co-exist. Simplicius[1], however, replied that the ἀταξία represents, not a separate force, but an ever-present tendency which makes itself felt even in the midst of τάξις. There is, in fact, nothing in the *Timaeus* myth that can be regarded as existing in separation from anything else; all the solitary forces there at work are abstractions, separated by sheer reason from the environment of which they are a vital part, and without which they themselves could not exist.

A literal interpretation, indeed, would raise endless difficulties; the whole phraseology and arrangement seem to militate against it. We are met from the beginning with conceptions such as οὐσία, ταὐτόν, θάτερον, which take us right back to the logical analysis of the *Sophist*, and which we cannot possibly regard as material things. Again, the story never proceeds uninterruptedly to a conclusion. Instead of a narrator who sees clearly before his mind's eye a definite series of events, we have here, as it were, a photographer, who is continually presenting us with the same scene taken from different points of view. Thus, in the beginning[2], the body of the universe is presumably fashioned out of the four elements, whose existence is pre-supposed; later at 53 B, however, these elements themselves are represented as being shaped by the θεὸς εἴδεσί τε καὶ ἀριθμοῖς. Could this possibly be part of a story which depends on time-sequence for its intelligibility? Similar instances are

---

[1] Simplicius, commentary on this passage.   [2] 31 B.

to be found at 29 A and 30 A, where τὸ γεγονὸς and τὸ ὁρατὸν are introduced before any γένεσις has taken place, and at 34 B and C, where we are told in almost the same breath that ψυχὴ is created within body (as if body were prior), and also that σῶμα is in no sense to be counted prior to ψυχή. Plato here, in fact, tells us plainly that he does not intend his words to be taken literally. Finally, of course, there is the insuperable difficulty, emphasised by Proclos, of explaining how time can be conceived of as being created as one of a series of creations all of which take place in time.

We may, then, I think, take it for granted that the myth of the *Timaeus* does not profess to describe any actual γένεσις of the world in time; and we shall be content to interpret γένεσις in the same sense as Plato himself, at 28 B, C, interprets it: that is, τὸ πᾶν is to be regarded as a γιγνόμενον, not because it has in any sense been produced at any special period, but because it belongs to the class of things, which, being objects of δόξα and αἴσθησις, are ever in flux and opposed to that which is truly ὄν. In this sense only Plato affirms that ὁ οὐρανὸς γέγονεν, and the problem he sets before himself in the *Timaeus* is two-fold: first, who or what is the αἰτία of this continual γένεσις, and secondly, what is the παράδειγμα in imitation of which it is framed, what is the eternal reality in virtue of which alone it retains such existence as it has? Our present object, then, will be to elicit from the poetical phraseology of the myth the result of Plato's deliberations on these two points.

In the beginning of his exposition Plato told us

4—2

that it would be hard to describe the αἰτία of the universe in any hard and fast language. He was content for the present simply to assume its existence and to call it the δημιουργός, the creator of all visible things. As the story proceeds, however, it is clear that the αἰτία may be regarded in two lights: it may be, first of all, the cause of motion, or of the actual γένεσις of phenomena, and, secondly, the final cause, the ideal " good " which is the end and aim of this γένεσις. The former aspect is unfolded in those passages [1] which represent the δημιουργός as the actual cause of becoming, and the communicator of motion to the bodily universe. The αἰτία as final cause is depicted chiefly in the descriptions [2] of the γένεσις of soul, where the δημιουργός is actuated by a beneficent purpose, and is practically identical with the idea of good, and especially at 41 A, where he supplies the soul-principle for the inferior animals, but declines to have any share in the creation of their bodies, or of the evil which they must necessarily encounter. The αἰτία here is obviously no movent cause, but, to quote Plato's own words, τῶν νοητῶν ἀεί τε ὄντων ἄριστον, the highest of ideal existences. He is νοήσει μετὰ λόγου περιληπτὸν [3] and μετὰ νοῦ καταφανές. He is, in short, to be identified with the supreme παράδειγμα itself.

In his character as the originator of motion the δημιουργός of the *Timaeus* would appear to be scarcely different from the ψυχὴ τοῦ κόσμου, which is consistently represented as having the cause of motion in herself (36 E), and as being the primary cause of motion in all other things (46 E). Plato is still true to his belief of

---

[1] 28 c ; 34 A.   [2] 29 E ; 37 A.   [3] 28 A.

the *Phaedo,* and more elaborate declaration in the
Philebus, that a divine νοῦς, an all-governing reason, is
the cause of all that is phenomenal. In words that
remind one most strongly of the *Phaedo* he affirms that
there are two kinds of causes, primary and secondary,
and whereas the latter embraces all manner of physical
processes, which most men regard as true causes, the
former sort is invisible, the direct activity of mind
and soul; and he that loves reason and knowledge
must seek the rational cause first, and the secondary
causes which transmit, but do not create motion, only
for the sake of the primary. We understand, therefore,
that mind and soul are the cause of the activity of the
universe no less than of human action and production;
we must postulate a universal mind and soul to govern
the infinite movement of the world. Everything that
Plato regards as necessary for the completion of the
universe is summed up at 47 E as τὰ διὰ νοῦ δεδημιουρ-
γημένα.

This view not only endorses the statement of the
Philebus already referred to, but is re-affirmed by the
well-known passage in the *Laws,* in which ψυχή [1], the
αὐτοκίνητος, is represented as the source of all the
γένεσις of the world. It has in itself the power of
moving, not only itself, but other things as well; all its
primary motions of βούλησις, βούλευσις, δόξα, and the
like, are reflected in the corporeal movements to which
they give rise. In the θεῖον γένος of the stars ψυχὴ as
ἀρχὴ κινήσεως is seen in its greatest perfection, for in
them νοῦς is least subject to the seductions of sense,
and their physical motions betoken the supreme regu-

[1] *Laws* 896 D, E. Cf. *Phaedrus* 245 c.

larity and precision of the soul-movements which they reflect.

There remains the larger question of the αἰτία as the final cause of the universe. Having satisfied ourselves that the movent cause is to be found in a universal ψυχή, we have still to seek its παράδειγμα, the idea or end for which it came into being. But before we undertake this new quest, it would be as well to have in mind the main features of this universe as Plato has sketched it [1]. It is a single, all-comprehensive animal, possessed of νοῦς and ψυχή as well as body, and containing all visible creatures that exist. Its body comprehends all fire, air, water and earth [2], so that nothing is left behind with which another σῶμα might be formed. It is ὅλον ἐξ ὅλων ἁπάντων, possessing no organs of sense, and therefore destitute of sensations except in so far as it may be said to have them through its various parts. Its shape is spherical, for the animal that contains within itself all possible animals should surely have that form which may be filled with all possible shapes, and its only motion is a revolution upon its own axis—that physical motion which approaches nearest to the pure activity of mind [3].

As regards its soul, one cannot be far wrong in ascribing to it, though in purer and more perfect proportions, a structure similar to that which one perceives in the ψυχαί of individual men. Ψυχή is a compound, formed of the οὐσία which is ἀμέριστος and ever changeless, and the οὐσία which is γιγνόμενον and divided in visible bodies, mingled with a third ingredient, Essence, which, like them, is a mixture of two

---

[1] 30 B.   [2] 32 D seq.   [3] Cf. *Laws* 898 A.

things, ταὐτὸν and θάτερον, and which, together with
these last, corresponds to one of the leading categories
of the *Sophist*, which are employed by the human mind
whenever she passes judgment on, or attains to knowledge of, anything whatsoever. A question arises here
as to Plato's exact meaning in saying that ψυχὴ is a compound of this sort, and that the changeless and changing
world, together with Essence, are composed of these two
ingredients, ταὐτὸν and θάτερον. The answer is surely
to be found at 37 A, B. There we find it clearly stated
that ψυχή, whenever she comes in contact with anything, whether it belongs to the class of the ἀμέριστον,
or that of the μεριστόν, being affected in her entire substance, tells that wherewith the thing is same, and that
wherefrom it is different. Hence we understand that
the function of ψυχή, whether it be that of cosmos or
individual, is to declare the relation of Same and Other
in regard to everything that comes under her operation,
whether it belong to the permanent and intelligible
sphere, or that of the sensible and ever-changing.
Ψυχὴ thus has the intelligible and sensible as ingredients because she deals with both alike, and these are
mingled with Essence, i.e., with Same and Other, inasmuch as these last are the leading predicates which she
necessarily employs in all her functioning. The whole
realm of ideas, moreover, and the sensible world of flux
likewise, are composed of Same and Other, inasmuch as
the mind is eternally decomposing them, different though
they be in kind, into these same two elements. In
fact, all existent things, so far as they are known,
may be said to consist of these ingredients.

This doctrine is not one that need surprise us here ;

it was stated before in a less explicit form in the
Sophist[1]. There, it will be remembered, the knowing
subject is said to have κοινωνία with τὸ γιγνόμενον by
means of αἴσθησις, and with τὸ ὄντως ὂν by means of
ψυχή, διὰ λογισμοῦ; here we have the theory of ψυχὴ
as a compound of the intelligible and the sensible. Also
the categories οὐσία, ταὐτόν, θάτερον and the like, are
found to have κοινωνία with one another in virtue of
their inherence in the same thing when analysed by
the same mind. Putting these two statements together, we arrive at the doctrine of the *Timaeus*. The
knowing subject, or, to borrow the language of the
Timaeus, the soul, in virtue of her κοινωνία with
the objects both of ἐπιστήμη and αἴσθησις, imparts
to both the attributes Same, Other and the like,
which are the universal predicates indispensable to
her activity, so that they may be said to consist of
these attributes. Hence the categories too, being
found in the same objects, have κοινωνία with one
another; and—a fact which is more important in the
light of one of the ἀπορίαι of the *Parmenides*—the
ideal world itself, consisting, in virtue of the κοινωνία
of ψυχή, of ταὐτόν, θάτερον and the rest, is capable of
receiving contrary attributes no less than the phenomenal: this, however, is no longer due to the κοινωνία
of incompatible ideal entities, but to the necessary
functioning of the mind, which, by participating in its
object, makes the object participate in all manner of
contradictory categories. Ideal and material worlds,
then, so far as they are *known*, may be said to consist of
Same and Other.

[1] *Sophist* 248 A.

THE WORLD-PROCESS OF THE TIMAEUS   57

But ψυχή, besides possessing Same and Other, and thereby Essence, as primary ingredients of her nature, has in addition the two motions, Same and Other, which apply respectively to the faculties of reason and sensation, inasmuch as reason is concerned with that which is κατὰ ταὐτὰ ἔχον, sensation with that which is continually θάτερον, γιγνόμενον καὶ ἀπολλύμενον (28 A). They are made to revolve after the fashion of the spheres of the fixed stars and planets, simply because Plato regards all physical motions as the counterpart of the noetic activity of νοῦς. Each of these circles, further, consists itself of Same and Other, for they are the essential modes of all activities of soul. Here we are in a position to realise even more perfectly why Plato should from the outset make the ἀμέριστον, which is νοητόν, and the μεριστόν, which is the object of sensation, ingredients in the formation of soul; soul partakes of the nature of both of these in virtue of her apprehension of both. One is reminded of the defini- tion of οὐσία which was introduced in the Sophist to satisfy Idealists and Materialists at once—ἡ δύναμις τοῦ ποιεῖν ἢ πάσχειν. Applied by the idealists, this definition included both οὐσία and ψυχή; applied by the materialists, it included both τὸ αἰσθητὸν and τὸ αἰσθανόμενον. Hence ψυχή, in any case, was to be counted οὐσία, inasmuch as it operated in both spheres. Plato, therefore, is still maintaining his compromise between materialism and idealism. Aware of the merits on both sides, he will not reject either utterly, and his conception of soul as the comprehensive essence, through which ideas and phenomena alike are appre- hended, and as the eternal cause to which phenomena owe their being, preserves the sovereignty of the ideal world, while accounting for the apparent reality of material things.

Besides functioning as reason and sensation and operating through Same and Other, the soul is represented as being composed of mathematical ratios, corresponding to the intervals of the diatonic scale. This of course signifies simply that the apprehension of harmony, too, is one of the striking modes of its operation. Soul, then, is not itself a harmony, as Simmias tried to hold in the *Phaedo*, but it has within it the power of grasping and understanding musical relations in virtue of number and proportion, which are indispensable modes of its activity.

In his account of ψυχή Plato has been enabled to lay down certain definite principles and to come to some definite conclusions. Concerning the body of the cosmos and its component parts, however, he cannot attain to certitude in any degree. It is ordained that everything which is visible shall be in eternal flux; consequently everything that goes to make up the material universe is subject to incessant variation of form. Not only do organisms suffer daily change within themselves, but they themselves in their entirety are forever passing away and being replaced by others, with the exception indeed of the stars, the heavenly bodies, who stand highest in the realm of creation, and in a peculiar way represent the universe itself, for they are its leading constituents, and from them is derived the substance of the smaller constituents. This, I think, is all that is meant by the creation by the θεοὶ θεῶν of mortal bodies. The individual souls of

men, animals, and all lower existences, receive their
bodily form from the planets, who are the firstborn of
the θεός, or rather, the highest phenomenal existences
in the universe. The fixed stars have already been
called into requisition to act as the ὀχήματα of the
souls while they listen to the Artificer's harangue
regarding the laws of the universe; and just as this
detail has a metaphorical significance merely, so the
creative function of the planets means simply that all
lower creatures derive their substance from the heavenly
bodies. Plato's language seems to me to admit of no
other interpretation. The δημιουργός himself is the
cause of the creation and differentiation of the souls;
what the θεοί do is simply to provide material for the
bodies, to nourish the bodies when made, and to
receive them again at death. Nothing can be gained
by attempting to extract an unnecessary complexity in
Plato's metaphysics from the picturesque scene in which
the δημιουργός, calling together the θεοὶ θεῶν, entrusts
to them the making of the bodies of inferior creatures.
But, to resume our account of the flux, part of the law
of change is that the inferior souls, which are parts of
the great soul, take upon them the nature of man, and
thereafter that of woman and the lower animals,
according to the merit or demerit of their successive
lives. The possession of body and sensation is an
unceasing source of temptation, and when a man is
mastered by the lower impulses of his soul, it is
ordained that his soul shall pass first into the body of
a woman, and, if even then he fails to repent of the
error of his way, into the form of some beast suited
to his particular nature. Only through following the

dictates of reason can he hope to escape, and rising
beyond the trammels of the body, return to his first
and best estate (πρὶν τῇ ταὐτοῦ καὶ ὁμοίου περιόδῳ τῇ
ἐν αὐτῷ ξυνεπισπόμενος τὸν πολὺν ὄχλον καὶ ὕστερον
προσφύντα ἐκ πυρὸς καὶ ὕδατος καὶ ἀέρος καὶ γῆς,
θορυβώδη καὶ ἄλογον ὄντα, λόγῳ κρατήσας εἰς τὸ τῆς
πρώτης καὶ ἀρίστης ἀφίκοιτο εἶδος ἕξεως. 42 D).

We have now reached a point where we may pause
to consider the nature of the idea or παράδειγμα,
which, Plato says, the δημιουργὸς had in view in the
production of a universe such as we have described·
That universe, fair though it be, is not calculated to
inspire the philosopher with satisfaction, for it is fated
to undergo incessant change, and the inferior souls
within it, by reason of their connexion with body, are
ever subject to misfortune. The world of sense is
unreal (28 A): it is an eternal illusion: it has in it
nothing akin to reason or thought (46 D): it only exists
in so far as it is seen or handled (31 B). Hence only
when a man's soul is free from sin, and thereby casts
off the incubus of body, will the illusion of sense cease
to have a meaning for him[1]; then his reason will work
in harmony with that of the All. How then are we to
describe the ideal permanency to which the δημιουργὸς
looked beyond all the flux of sense? It is τὸ τῶν νοουμένων κάλλιστον καὶ κατὰ πάντα τέλεον[2]. But it is before
all else a ζῷον, an eternal and perfect animal, which
contains within itself all other νοητὰ ζῷα that are.
Now a ζῷον, as Plato indicates time and again, is a
complex being possessing faculties both bodily and
mental; but if a ζῷον is to be νοητὸν merely, if it is to

[1] 42 D.   [2] 30 D.

be placed in the category of the changeless and eternal, it must assuredly, on Platonic principles, divest itself of everything that is perceptible, of all those attributes which cling to it in virtue of its bodily nature. As a result of this process it becomes not even ψυχή (since ψυχή, too, in this dialogue, is concerned in part with bodily functions), but νοῦς pure and simple. As the Kebes of the *Phaedo* puts it : ὅλῳ καὶ παντὶ ὁμοιότερόν ἐστι ψυχὴ τῷ ἀεὶ ὡσαύτως ἔχοντι μᾶλλον ἢ τῷ μή[1].

The supreme παράδειγμα of the universe, then, being a ζῷον and a νοητὸν ζῷον, is νοῦς, a perfect universal νοῦς; and the ideas of the subordinate creatures are only μόρια καθ' ἓν καὶ κατὰ γένη of the αὐτὸ ὃ ἔστι ζῷον[2]. At 39 E Plato says: "As many kinds as mind perceives to exist in the αὐτὸ ζῷον, so many did the δημιουργὸς think fit that the visible world should contain, and of these there are in the main four kinds, first, the heavenly deities, and after them the tribes that inhabit the air, the water, and the earth." This statement translated into ordinary language means that only the animal creation, the various tribes that inhabit the four elements, merit ideal counterparts and a share in the αὐτὸ ζῷον, the consummation of all existence. Now this restriction of ideas to the various species of animals carries our thoughts at once to the transmigration theory, and the fact that within all these tribes, from man downwards, there is a constant struggle between higher and lower impulses, with the result that the individual soul is continually being reincarnated in a higher or a lower form. The animals for whom ideas are reserved are exactly those who come

[1] *Phaedo* 79 E.   [2] 30 c.

within the range of transmigration, the tribes of air, earth and sea, each of which, according to Plato, represents the souls of mortal men which have degenerated through the taint of sin. It is true, of course, that the heavenly deities, who are immeasurably removed from human frailty and the need of transmigration alike, are also mentioned ; but Plato has so often emphasised their pre-eminence, and their close connexion with the All itself, that one is not surprised to find them at the head of the ideas here. They assuredly will have their counterpart in the ideal sphere, for they of all material things are the most perfect imitators of Reason. The members of the vegetable kingdom, on the other hand, which at first sight would not seem to enter into the scheme of transmigration, have no place in the list of ideas as here given. Plato, however, acknowledged them to be ζῷa of a kind, and he must inevitably in drawing up a complete list of ideas have included them both in his system of transmigration and of ideas. Empedocles, his predecessor in the transmigration-doctrine, not only made plants participate in the process of metempsychosis. but affirmed that he himself had been a θάμνος.

It would appear, therefore, that the scheme of ideas as here propounded has its basis in ethics. The tribes of the air, earth, and sea are assigned a share in the αὐτὸ ζῷον because they are degenerate forms of the immortal principle of soul, which when it is conceived as functioning in perfect purity and unity, like the ἀληθινὸς καὶ θεῖος νοῦς of *Philebus* 22 c, is the ideal ζῷον itself. It is only the body, and the sensations and lusts that attend upon it, that keep the individual ψυχή from functioning in harmony with that of the All; they inflict upon it harder and harder penalties in proportion to its weakness, and prevent the realisation of that ideal universe, an all-embracing mind, working in unison with itself as one whole, perfect and undivided. The beasts of the field, then, the fowls of the air, and the fish of the sea, have each in their kind a share in the ideal ζῶον, for they represent a portion of the universal soul, which is ever constant, though subject to the adverse power of sin: and the eternal prototype of each is simply a specific or generic determination, as the case may be, of the universal νοῦς, which is the supreme idea and παράδειγμα, the ultimate goal of all human endeavour. In other words, Plato here indicates that the ideas, which have for so long been the cardinal principle of his ontology, are in the last analysis special modes of regarding a universal νοῦς, for the realisation of which every soul, albeit unconsciously, strives, the final end and purpose of that everlasting process of which the world-soul is the cause —the world-soul itself conceived in its highest phase and measured by its highest achievement. Thus the idea of star is simply one aspect of the universal νοῦς, which must be considered as providing the type for the soul-activity of the stars, and of every soul throughout the whole range of living genera and species, and also, secondarily and indirectly, as being the cause of everything that is καλὸν in the visible world. Even in the *Sophist* Plato repudiated the thought that τὸ παντελῶς ὂν[1] could be devoid of ζωή; and these εἴδη are confined to ζῶα alone. No room for in-

[1] *Sophist* 249 A.

animate objects can possibly be made in the four-
fold classification of 40 A without forcing the language
beyond measure. The position which Plato assigns to
inanimate substances, such as the four elements, and
the nature of the ideas of these, will be defined when
we come to our examination of the physical portion of
the *Timaeus*.

Priority in time in the myth stands, as we have
shown above, for priority in ideal importance, and
when Plato speaks of a man, after many transmigrations
and much conflict with bodily passion, attaining to his
first and best nature, we may be sure that the first and
best nature is that which is ideally and eternally first,
though not in time. Hence the journey by which the
soul is freed from bodily hindrance, and learns to
function in harmony with the great soul of the universe, is not strictly a " return " in time, but the much-
wished-for and well-nigh unrealisable ideal of the
philosopher. If every soul were to attain to its first
estate, then the supreme idea would be perfectly
represented in time, and Plato is not without hope
that some souls at least may pass beyond the reach of
bodily hindrance and evil [1]. The soul of him who is free
from bodily ills will be given a place on its kindred
star and learn the nature of the universe as it truly is,
like the souls of those who, in the *Phaedrus*, viewed
the ideas in the supracelestial region. For Plato's
θεòς is not a God, who literally creates, in the
beginning, a universe that is altogether fair and good,
and souls whom no spot of imperfection has yet
touched; it is the eternal idea, for which the whole

[1] 42 c, d ; 44 c ; 90 d.

creation yearns, and strives through many imperfections to reach, and towards which every achievement of the intellect, every victory gained by soul over body, is an advance.

To sum up the metaphysical significance of the world-process which we have been reviewing, Plato seems in the first portion of the *Timaeus* to have enunciated in a poetical form the leading features of his latest view of the universe. From the first he felt sure that there was some permanent principle or principles underlying variable phenomena. He has made diligent search for it, and, as his declarations in the *Phaedo, Philebus*, and *Sophist* would lead us to expect, he has found it in soul and mind. Reason is the highest and best thing of which the human being has experience, hence to nothing less than reason can he attribute the perfection and ultimate reality of everything he sees. Even physical motion is but the material counterpart of noetic activity; and time, which measures all physical motion and change, is but the image of eternity, throughout which the activity of supreme νοῦς endures.

And Reason has two aspects; it is both αἰτία and παράδειγμα, of which the latter is prior in logical and ideal importance. The source of existence is in its highest phase the source of good, as the teaching of the *Republic* leads us to expect. To the universal soul man owes his very existence, and he must forever seek and emulate it in its divine and ideal form, if he is to gain a happy life. When every soul in the universe has become attuned to the harmony of the universal νοῦς, and has cast off all that burden of earth and fire

and water, which clung to it in virtue of the faculties
of sense, then, and not till then, will come the perfect
representation in time of the supreme idea of the universe, and the various ideas of animal life of which it is
composed.   And, if ever the individual intellect is thus
exalted, it shall know and realise for the first time true
beauty and justice and knowledge, that aspect of the
ideal world that impressed itself first on Plato's mind[1].
Those eternal essences, which were the load-star of his
early ambitions, have now found a resting-place worthy
of their exalted rank.   We saw that one of the chief
results of the *Parmenides* was the conviction that the
ideas and the supreme idea, if they are to be not merely
existent, but objects of knowledge, must have real and
lasting connexion with one another as well as with the
flux of sense.   Here, then, in the *Timaeus*, we find
this condition fulfilled ; the ideas stand to the supreme
idea in the most intimate of relations: they are aspects
of the perfect and all-sufficient νοῦς, which is brought
into vital contact with the souls of all the generic and
specific forms of life.

Finally, may we not say that Plato has in this
dialogue amply satisfied the criteria furnished by the
criticism of the *Parmenides* and *Sophist* ?   The supreme
ἕν, if it is to be known, must exist not in self-identity
merely, but in relation to the many too.   Further, in
the *Sophist* it was found that it must possess κίνησις,
ζωή, νοῦς and ψυχή.   We are now assured that the
θεῖος νοῦς *is* the supreme ἕν, that it has life and
activity, and that only in so far as they imitate it
successfully can the individual souls be said to possess
reality at all.

[1] Cf. *Phaedo* 114 c.

ESSAY IV.

THE IDEAS AS Ἀριθμοί.

THE portion of the *Timaeus* with which we must now deal forms a contrast in many respects to the former half, which we have just left. The object of the earlier chapters was not so much to describe to us the cosmos in its material aspect, as to unveil to us its ideal prototype, and to take us to the very source of all its activities, to discover to us a universal and eternal νοῦς, which manifests itself in the cosmos just as surely as our minds find expression in our bodies, and which, when conceived of as functioning in unrestrained perfection, is the ethical ideal in imitation of which the world, with all the creatures contained therein, was created. From 47 E onwards, however, Plato addresses himself to the task of examining the material universe itself, in the hope of laying down, if possible, certain definite principles, which may be said to govern the operations of the universal soul in the visible world. Having given dogmatic utterance to his conviction that νοῦς and ψυχή are the ultimate cause of all phenomenal things, he now endeavours to support it by a minute examination of phenomena. His attitude, therefore, has changed;

all his attention is now directed towards the material
universe itself, in order that he may find therein the
proof of the belief that he has just proclaimed.   This is,
indeed, the only course open to him; it is inevitable
that he should begin with the world of time and space,
in which he finds himself.   It is only through using
material objects as images that we may hope to assume
the existence of the ideas, which are the goal of all
knowledge.   If we would try from the outset to look
straight at the sun, we should only make for ourselves
darkness through excess of light.

Plato, accordingly, begins this second part of the
dialogue by declaring his intention of retracing his
steps in order to set forth the nature of ἀνάγκη and the
πλανωμένη αἰτία, which share with νοῦς the responsi-
bility for the material order of things.   In particular,
he is desirous of enquiring into the nature of air, earth,
fire, and water, whose existence was assumed from the
first as being essential to the materiality of the universe,
but of which no explanation has yet been given.   This
new method and point of view necessitate a fresh
classification of existence, based upon a different principle
of division.   Instead of having two classes, the νοητὸν
and the ὁρατόν, the παράδειγμα and the μίμημα, we
now have three, viz., the νοητόν, the ὁρατόν, and the
ὑποδοχὴ γενέσεως, an εἶδος which is χαλεπὸν and
ἀμυδρόν.   To define this latter, the Substrate of
Becoming, is an extremely difficult task.   Its nature can
scarcely be expressed in positive language; in fact, it
cannot be described at all without calling to our aid the
phenomena of which it is the receptacle.   Now we see
that fire, water, and all substances that are possessed of

sensible qualities, are forever in a process of trans-
mutation ; water is continually changing into earth or
air, and air in turn becomes fire ; the flux is ceaseless,
and it is impossible to call any of these bodies by any
definite term, since one is never sure that it has not
already become different. But one may conceive of
something *in which* all these varying phenomena arise,
and to which, in virtue of its permanence, a name may
safely be assigned. In order to understand the nature
of this receptacle we may take the illustration of gold,
which in the hands of the craftsman takes upon itself
in turn all manner of forms and shapes, but which in
strictness can be termed gold and nothing else. In like
manner the ὑποδοχή receives within itself all material
bodies, and puts on all manner of varying appearances,
while it is itself utterly devoid of body or form. This
is its sole function, and it is eternally true to that
function. The ever-varying bodies that enter into it
are likenesses of eternal existences, copied from them in
a strange and mysterious fashion which will hereafter
be explained. Meantime we are satisfied that the
universe may be said to consist of three kinds : τὸ
γιγνόμενον, τὸ ἐν ᾧ γίγνεται, and τὸ δ' ὅθεν ἀφομοιούμενον
φύεται τὸ γιγνόμενον.

Here Plato pauses to answer a supposed objection.
Are you right in mentioning likenesses and models in
this connexion ? Is there, for example, such a thing as
πῦρ ἐφ' ἑαυτοῦ, the likenesses of which enter into the
ὑποδοχή ? And are there ideas of all the other bodies
which we have been calling μιμήματα τῶν ἀεὶ ὄντων ?
The answer is decisive. If νοῦς and δόξα ἀληθής are
to be eternally distinct, then assuredly there are ideas

of this kind, entirely separate from the sensible objects
which we perceive, ἀναίσθητα ὑφ᾽ ἡμῶν εἴδη, νοούμενα
μόνον. We therefore re-affirm our classification. There
is, first, the invisible and immutable idea, to be grasped
by νόησις alone, secondly, its copy, which is subject to
ceaseless flux, and apprehended by αἴσθησις, and,
thirdly, eternal χώρα, the ἕδρα of all Becoming, which
is grasped λογισμῷ τινι νοθῷ. It is this χώρα, adds
Plato, which is always perverting our judgment when
we are considering immaterial things. Because a
material body, being a perishable copy, must perforce
arise in something, in order to come into existence at
all, we must needs apply spatial relations to the ideal
world too; whereas reason should tell us that the natures
of idea and copy are so essentially distinct that the
conditions of the one are in no wise applicable to the
other.

Proceeding with his analysis, Plato goes on to say
that the ὑποδοχή, being ceaselessly filled with earth, air,
fire and water, is continually disturbed, and is subject
to a vibratory motion due to the diversity and inequality
of the bodies which enter into it. This vibration reacts
also upon the objects by which it is caused, and has the
effect of separating and sifting them, so that similar
things are gradually drawn together.

We have now to learn the explanation of the
generation of fire and the other elements, which we
were led to expect at 50 C. In order to make them as
fair as possible, the creator from the first shaped them
with forms and numbers. Now, seeing that they are
material bodies, and that material bodies require depth
and therefore surface, it is plain that these elements

have surface, of which the simplest example is the triangle ; and all triangles may be resolved into two, the rectangular isosceles and the rectangular scalene, which we accordingly affirm to be the bases of the elements, although we acknowledge that there may be ἀρχαί even beyond these, known to God alone, and such as are friends of God. Our task now is to choose the figure appropriate to each element, and to decide upon the ἀριθμοί or proportions in which the constituent triangles are combined (οἷον δὲ ἕκαστον αὐτῶν γέγονεν εἶδος καὶ ἐξ ὅσων συμπεσόντων ἀριθμῶν[1]). To begin with fire, we find that six rectangular scalenes combine to form an equilateral triangle, four of which may be placed together to form the first regular solid, the pyramid. This figure we conceive to be the typical form of fire, and we may therefore say that fire is composed of six primal scalenes combined together four times, or a total of twenty-four primal scalenes. The form of air is the octahedron, and is made up of six multiplied by eight, or forty-eight primal scalenes. Water, which is represented by the icosahedron, is composed of 6×20, or 120, of the same primal triangles. These three elements, being all capable of transformation into one another, are accordingly furnished with the same base. Earth, which stands apart from them, has as its element the rectangular isosceles, which, when combined in six sets of four, gives rise to the cube, the εἶδος of earth. Earth, then, is formed of 4×6, or 24, of the rectangular isosceles triangles.

This apportioning of the regular solids to the different elements is justified by a comparison of the

[1] 54 D.

attributes of the figures with those of the elements
they denote. As earth is the most stable of elements,
so the equilateral triangle and the square are the most
stable of plane, and the cube of solid, figures. Fire too,
being the keenest of the four elements, is well represented by the pyramid, which is the sharpest of solid
figures.

These, then, being the figures of which fire, air,
earth and water are constituted, we must first conceive
of each of them as being in isolation too small to affect
the eye; only when gathered together in great multi-
tudes can they be supposed to give any impression of
magnitude. Next, all these bodies, three of which
may have ceaseless generation into one another, must
be regarded as continually changing their positions,
owing to the vibration of the ὑποδοχή, and as being
inevitably carried towards the others of their own kind,
inasmuch as similar things are always attracted towards one another, and there is no arbitrary distinction
of "up" and "down." In the course of this vibration
and attraction it may happen that the octahedrons of
air, or the icosahedrons of water, become divided by
the keenness of the pyramids of fire, and the octahedron
thus changes into two particles of fire, and the icosahedron becomes one particle of fire and two of air. Earth,
however, can only be dissolved into its parts, which
thereupon drift about till they can be united once more.
But on this principle alone it would seem that kindred
particles would speedily become associated, and all need
of further disintegration would cease. There is, accordingly, another force at work, which prevents such stag-
nation, viz., ἡ τοῦ παντὸς περίοδος, which compresses the

matter of the universe with such all-pervading force that
no intervals are suffered to remain between the kinds,
and consequently one is continually being compelled to
interpenetrate the other. These two forces, then, the
vibration of the ὑποδοχή, and the πίλησις of the
revolving universe, combine to produce eternal movement and disturbance among the kinds.

The remainder of the dialogue is occupied by a
minute examination of all the kinds that arise by
combination of these four elements, together with
a physiological analysis of the senses and the bodily
functions. Within the elements themselves, we are
told, there are distinct γένη, which owe their variety to
differences of size in the primal triangles of which they
are composed. But, apart from these, there are in-
numerable compound substances, such as stone, earthen-
ware, salt, formed of different proportions of the four
elements. Animal and vegetable bodies, both in whole
and in part, arise out of one or other combination of
fire, air, earth and water[1]. Marrow, bone, flesh and
sinew are all compounded in this fashion[2]. Everything
in the universe, in fact, as far as its materiality is
concerned, may be built up out of fixed proportions of
these ingredients.

It is now time to turn back and follow up the course
of Plato's argument in order to set down in plain
language the results at which he has been aiming. If
we are to take 50 c seriously, Plato's intention has
been to show us in some measure how the εἰσιόντα
καὶ ἐξιόντα, the ever-varying flux of phenomena, may
be regarded as the representatives in space of im-

[1] 73 B–E.   [2] 74 C, D.

mutable εἴδη, which exist eternally and are independent
of actual relation to space and time. Our object then
must be, first, to come to some understanding concerning the ὑποδοχή, in which phenomena are said
to arise, and, secondly, to discover the nature of the
εἴδη of fire, etc., which are introduced in such an
emphatic way at 51 B. We shall then be in a position
to draw some conclusions regarding the aim and objects
of knowledge, according to Plato's latest utterance on
the subject.

Those who would interpret the *Timaeus* literally
seem to be disposed to treat the ὑποδοχή as an actual
κενόν, or void, like that of Democritus, in which
actual atoms did, at some prehistoric period or other,
float about in the way described. This view is of
course excluded by our general treatment of the
dialogue, but there are besides two serious considerations that make it absolutely impossible to hold it for
a moment. First of all, one cannot conceive of Plato
as being willing to imitate the Atomists after the
wholesale contempt which he has poured upon them,
not only in previous dialogues, but in the *Timaeus*
itself[1]. The open enemy of the Atomists is not likely
to adopt their materialistic bases and automatic processes in trying to account for an orderly world. Secondly,
the whole development of the conception of the ὑποδοχὴ is opposed to any such view. Plato is obviously
taking the material world as it is, and gradually
abstracting from it everything of a bodily nature.
The κενὸν is an abstract conception, which is reached
only after laborious thought; it is not, like that of

[1] See 46 D; 55 D. Cf. *Soph.* 265 c, D.

Democritus, assumed as the primary condition of the universe. From pages 49 A to 51 B, which are devoted entirely to the gradual unfolding of the notion of χώρα, we learn that it is that which remains of the material world when it is divested of all body, shape and quality. It is that underlying principle which remains permanent amid their everlasting mutability, and may be illustrated by the example of gold, upon which all manner of shapes are continually impressed and as continually obliterated. It is plain that Plato's whole endeavour here is to get a firm grasp of the notion of space by abstraction, for he can only conceive of it by ridding his mind of the actual world he sees. So far from describing a material process from space and atoms to actual existence, he presents us here with a logical progression from actual existence to space and the geometrical elements.

What then is the nature of this χώρα, when it has at length been reached? Enough has been said to show that it was not intended for an actually existent void. Let us, therefore, try to elicit from Plato's further treatment of the subject some information regarding its nature. Plato, having conceived the notion of the substrate, immediately fills it with certain elementary triangles, which combine in certain fixed modes to form figures, which are the ἀρχαί of the four elements and their combinations. Χώρα also allows of the activity of certain forces, which unite to keep the ἀρχαί in a state of continual disturbance. Now, these τρίγωνα are manifestly the plane triangles of geometry, the perfect, ideal triangles which the crude triangles of our diagrams affect to represent,

the ἀεὶ ὄντα of *Republic* 527 B, which are a stepping-
stone in our mental progress towards the ἰδέα τἀγαθοῦ.
This conclusion is not only the natural inference from
Plato's express statement at 53 C, where he makes it
perfectly plain that the geometrical laws conditioning
the perception of solids are his sole consideration, but
it is the only explanation that tallies with the details of
Plato's exposition.   Mr Archer-Hind, at pp. 203, 204
of his edition of the *Timaeus*, has pointed out that no
solid bodies could fulfil the requirements made for the
pyramids, octahedrons, and other figures in c. 22.   Two
solid pyramids could not possibly be transmuted into
a solid octahedron, but, according to the geometrical
law regulating pyramids and octahedrons, two pyramids consist of eight equal planes, and thus supply all
that is theoretically necessary to the constitution of an
octahedron.

The triangular planes, then, and the figures alike
are to be conceived of as the ideal triangles and figures
of geometrical definition, the perfect and immutable
laws which form the foundation of the sciences called
geometry and stereometry.   They are eternal and
immutable, in contradistinction to phenomenal things
which are apprehensible by the senses alone; and yet
they are πολλά, inasmuch as their multiplication is
theoretically essential to the production of more advanced figures.   These, then, are the σχήματα which
Plato's ὑποδοχή is destined to contain, and, difficult
though it be to define its nature, we are assured
that our explanation of it must be consistent with
the nature of the τρίγωνα, and the more complex
εἴδη, which it is made to contain.   It is, accordingly,

impossible either to regard the ὑποδοχὴ as an actual void, or to connect it directly with the world of γιγνόμενα at all; Plato has indeed taken great pains to divest it of all trace of the phenomenal. It is an ideal χώρα, the χώρα which is logically necessary for the operations of the ideal τρίγωνα and πυραμίδες of true geometry; it is a χώρα which exists in the mind alone, λόγῳ περιληπτόν.

It will be remembered that we noticed some attempt at a similar analysis in the *Philebus*. There Plato conceived of the ὕλη ἐξ οὗ γίγνεται τὸ πᾶν as sensible qualities, abstracted from the objects in which they were made to inhere by the mind. But the distinction between the ὕλη ἐξ οὗ and the ὕλη ἐν ᾧ was evidently unconsciously present to his mind, for he spoke of a ἕδρα, in which these qualities (τὸ μᾶλλόν τε καὶ ἧττον) arise, so that in the background of his thoughts there was evidently the notion of a ὕλη ἐν ᾧ as well as of a ὕλη ἐξ οὗ. In the *Timaeus* the sensible qualities, the ὕλη ἐξ οὗ, have been entirely superseded. Plato seems to have become more and more convinced of their relative and secondary character. At 61 E ff. he informs us that all such qualities are simply the varying effects which the different structures of the elements make upon our senses. He appears to have examined these qualities, and to have discovered that they may all ultimately be reduced to two, or rather that they all depend ultimately upon the principle of two, viz., τὸ μεῖζον καὶ σμικρότερον. Spatial extension and size are the fundamental attributes of everything bodily, and accordingly we may in our present examination discard ὕλη ἐξ οὗ, and concentrate our attention upon ὕλη ἐν ᾧ. It may be noted that Aristotle[1], ignoring Plato's ultimate rejection of antithetical qualities as ὕλη, chose out hot and cold, wet and dry, as the proximate ὕλη of material bodies, probably in imitation of the *Philebus*. The τρίγωνα of the *Timaeus* were not calculated to appeal to his practical turn of mind.

As Plotinus[2] indicates in the *Enneads*, one thing may be said to be in another quite apart from any question of spatial relation, just as many things in here in mind, and hence the ὑποδοχὴ possesses only a φάντασμα of ὄγκος. From chapter 20 onwards, therefore, we have before us the conception of geometrical space, containing within itself the ἀΐδια τρίγωνα, and the figures formed of these, which are the ideal counterparts of the four elements of the universe; and these ἀρχαὶ inhere in it not in a state of rest, but they are evermore subject to two forces, which Plato felt to be at work in the material universe. The vibration and the πίλησις, too, have been abstracted from the confusion of the visible objects which they are seen to affect, and transferred to a geometrical region where their operations may be viewed in the clear light of the intellect, and set down in fixed and unambiguous formulae. One is forcibly reminded of the ὃν τάχος and the οὖσα βραδυτὴς of *Republic* 529 D, also of the true heavens, wherein there moved true stars. Plato's whole object in this exposition of physical phenomena has been to arrive at exactitude of some kind, to be able to state in some fixed language the principles of order that underlie

---

[1] See Ar. *de gen. et corr.* B. 1. 329 ᵃ 24 ; 2. 329 ᵇ 7 ; 3. 330 ᵃ 30.
[2] Plotinus, *Enneads* ii. 4. 11 (xii. 11 Kirchhoff).

the γιγνόμενα of the universe. Hence the whole totality of physical γένεσις has been translated into ideal being in terms of mathematical and geometrical relations.

If this be so, what are we to say about the ideas of fire, etc., to which special attention was drawn at 51 B? In considering this question we should bear in mind continually the fact that Plato's point of view has changed since we last heard of ideas at 39 E, and that the three-fold classification into ὄν, γιγνόμενον, and ὑποδοχή must needs affect to some extent our view of τὸ ὄν. For τὸ ὄν is now the father, and χώρα the mother, of γένεσις; the idea is not wholly responsible for its copies, but must enter into relation with χώρα for their production. The idea, accordingly, must be expressed in such terms as would render the simile appropriate. The function of the ὑποδοχή is to afford room for γένεσις; it is the recipient of all that is spatial; the idea, then, must be conceived as far as possible in terms consistent with spatial relation. Plato, immediately after he has affirmed the existence of ideas of fire and the rest, proceeds to give an account of the διάταξις, or arrangement, of each of these bodies. Fire, it is discovered, has as its intelligible ἀρχή the pyramid, and the pyramid is inevitably composed of four sets of six primal scalene triangles. Similarly, the octahedron and the icosahedron, being the ἀρχαί of air and water respectively, are the result of the combination of eight, and twenty, sets of six primal scalenes. Earth has for its ἀρχή the cube, to compose which six sets of four rectangular isosceles triangles are always required. Thus the law governing fire-formation is that 24, or 6 × 4, primal scalenes shall combine to form a pyramid, the

ἀρχή of fire. Air, water, and earth are likewise subject
to similar laws; and Plato, by taking up every variety
of material body and substance in turn, might have
found similar laws to regulate them all. In the case of
stone, flesh, bone, and the like, he has shown us how
the principle works out. The more complex structures
of the bodies of animals, however, have not been
directly dealt with, but that Plato conceived them too
to be composed of primary triangles combined in
varying ways is obvious throughout the physiological
discourse.

These material laws, then, that govern all the kinds
within the material universe, I hold to be the εἴδη ἐφ'
ἑαυτῶν mentioned at 51 B. Such a view finds confirmation from many sources. First, one cannot but feel that
material bodies such as fire, air, water and earth, and
their combinations, which exist simply to be perceived
by sight and touch[1], and are mere modes of matter,
stand on quite a different footing from the ζῶα, that
have within them the very principle of life, and should,
therefore, receive a different treatment. We cannot,
accordingly, include these ideas of fire and the like
among the first-mentioned ideas of 39 E, the νοητὰ ζῶα,
which were special aspects of the supreme and ever-
active νοῦς. At the same time, though the elements
are not as intimately connected as the ζῶα with the
great αἰτία, νοῦς, that underlies all phenomena, they
are none the less eternal manifestations of noetic force.
The θεὸς made them fair, and brought them into order
according to definite and eternal laws. These laws,
therefore, are not unworthy of the title of εἴδη; they

[1] 31 B.

are unbegotten, imperishable, invisible, objects of thought alone.

Secondly, our investigation of the *Philebus* resulted in the conviction that the ideas there were to be found in the class of μέτρια, the eternal laws of proportion, which depend for their realisation on mathematical ποσά. All existing μικτά, we found, could be resolved into two elements, of which the ὕλη of sensible qualities was one, and the ideal law of proportion the other, while universal νοῦς, as αἰτία τῆς μίξεως, was the reality yet further back to which their existence could be traced.

A third confirmation lies in the fact that the εἴδη as ἀριθμοὶ were a phase of the ideas which attained considerable importance in the later days of Plato's school, and which was always said by Aristotle to have originated in the teaching of the master himself, in spite of all the accretions of the Platonists that tended to obscure it. A minute analysis of the evidence on this point awaits us in a later paper; but it is quite clear that these formative laws are nothing else but ἀριθμοί. Each εἶδος is said to consist of definite ἀριθμοί, or proportions, of primary triangles, and Plato himself uses the word twice in his exposition of the subject (εἴδεσί τε καὶ ἀριθμοῖς, 53 B; ἐξ ὅσων συμπεσόντων ἀριθμῶν, 54 D). All these chapters, indeed, breathe the spirit of the mathematician. Never since the *Republic* has Plato given the subject so much attention, or assigned to it so lofty a function.

Finally, have we now reached the limit of human knowledge? From the first the εἴδη ἐφ' ἑαυτῶν were to be objects of human knowledge, and now the possibility

w.   6

of knowing them has been realised beyond dispute.
But are we to stop there? Are we to be content with
knowing the fixities inherent in matter, eternal and
immutable though they be, and never penetrate
further? We were told in the earlier part of the
Timaeus that there was an ultimate αἰτία for all
Becoming, a παράδειγμα for all creation. Is this ever
to be known or realised? There are considerations
which seem to show that Plato did not despair of
attaining even this ambition. It must be remembered
that Plato has been trying to work back to the
subjective ἀρχαὶ of matter, and has reduced the
various material kinds to the primary notions on
which our apprehension of them, as matter, depends.
After all, ἀριθμοί, though they prove to us the presence
of νοῦς in the world, are not in themselves ultimate;
number is simply a necessity of our mind, as essential to
its working as the categories of Same and Other. Hence
Plato, in resolving matter into ἀριθμοί, has resolved it
into its subjective factors, thereby taking us to the
limit of the analysis the finite mind can reach. May
mind, *quâ* infinite, go a step further, and pass beyond
the subjective ἀρχαὶ to the absolute ἀρχὴ of all? At
53 D we are told: τὰς δ' ἔτι τούτων ἀρχὰς ἄνωθεν θεὸς
οἶδε, καὶ ἀνδρῶν ὃς ἂν ἐκείνῳ φίλος ᾖ. In this we can
only see a hope that the human mind may some time,
somehow, through a diligent pursuit of the εἴδη as
ἀριθμοί, rise to a still higher form of knowledge, and
know by direct intuition the νοητὸν ζῷον and the
νοητὰ ζῷα, which represent the ideal in its highest
form. As in the *Republic*, ἀριθμοὶ are to be the
stepping-stones to the realisation of the Good; but the

ἀριθμοί have now a greater importance than formerly, since they represent the highest actual point which human knowledge has yet reached. Διὸ δή, says Plato, χρὴ δύ' αἰτίας εἴδη διορίζεσθαι, τὸ μὲν ἀναγκαῖον, τὸ δὲ θεῖον, καὶ τὸ μὲν θεῖον ἐν ἅπασι ζητεῖν κτήσεως ἕνεκα εὐδαίμονος βίου, καθ' ὅσον ἡμῶν ἡ φύσις ἐνδέχεται, τὸ δὲ ἀναγκαῖον ἐκείνων χάριν, λογιζόμενον, ὡς ἄνευ τούτων οὐ δυνατὰ αὐτὰ ἐκεῖνα, ἐφ' οἷς σπουδάζομεν, μόνα κατανοεῖν, οὐδ' αὖ λαβεῖν, οὐδ' ἄλλως πως μετασχεῖν. (68 E—69 A[1].)

Before we conclude the subject of the ἀριθμοί, there are two points which would seem to demand some further elucidation. The first is concerned with the objective reality of space. We realise that the χώρα of the *Timaeus* is not an actual void, but an ideal, mathematical χώρα. May we then draw any conclusion as to whether Plato considered space to have independent existence, or whether it was to him a mere illusion? Here, of course, one feels the inappropriateness of making Plato speak in Berkeleian phraseology, and yet it is impossible to suppose him to believe that space was anything in itself. The whole universe, and time too, are always but shadows that appeal to the senses alone. Fire, air, water, and earth, which constitute the material universe, only exist for the sake of being seen. Qualities, which, after all, are what we have most in mind when we allude to the material world, are just affections of our senses, caused by something, it is true, but by something of alien nature to the things we see. When one divests the universe of these qualities, one has left indeed the ὑποδοχὴ γενέσεως, the δύναμις of γένεσις, within which

[1] Cf. 59, 60.

84   THE IDEAS AS 'Αριθμοί

to reconstruct ideally the eternal principles of matter,
but this has no objective existence; it is a φάντασμα.
With the reduction of qualities to their subjective
factors, one rejects the independent reality of the whole
material universe, and consequently of extension too,
for extension can never have actual existence apart
from extended objects.

The second subject referred to is that of the εἰσιόντα
καὶ ἐξιόντα, which have usually been identified[1] with
the μαθηματικά, or τρίγωνα, of c. 20. This identification
I believe to be impossible for the following reasons. In
the first place, there is nothing whatever in the actual
context of 50 C to lead one to associate the εἰσιόντα
καὶ ἐξιόντα with μαθηματικὰ at all. There has as yet
been no mention of geometrical forms. Plato's sole
aim here is to reach a conception of pure space by
stripping the world of every visible and variable
quality. Space is that ἐν ᾧ ἐγγιγνόμενα ἀεὶ ἕκαστα
αὐτῶν φαντάζεται καὶ πάλιν ἐκεῖθεν ἀπόλλυται[2]. It is
ἡ τὰ πάντα δεχομένη σώματα φύσις[3], which nevertheless
μορφὴν οὐδεμίαν ποτὲ οὐδενὶ τῶν εἰσιόντων ὁμοίαν
εἴληφεν οὐδαμῇ οὐδαμῶς[4]. Hence it is not a question of
triangles at all, but of γιγνόμενα, which are in continual
flux.

Secondly, the triangles are not εἰσιόντα καὶ ἐξιόντα;
they do not come into being and vanish, for they are
regarded as filling up every nook and cranny of the
ὑποδοχή, so that void may be as far as possible non-
existent. To this it may be replied that the particular
combinations of triangles—pyramids, octahedrons, and

---
[1] e.g. Adam's *Republic*, vol. ii. p. 161.
[2] 49 E.   [3] 50 B.   [4] 50 C.

the rest—come and vanish; but even so the ὑποδοχὴ does not rid itself of μαθηματικά, the constituent triangles being always constant[1], and the cube does not suffer destruction at all. How could the εἰσιόντα καὶ ἐξιόντα, which are admittedly always coming and going, be identical with μαθηματικά, or the πέρας ἔχοντα of the *Philebus*, which are directly opposed to that which is in flux? The εἰσιόντα καὶ ἐξιόντα are akin, if to anything, to the ἄπειρα, which are subject to unceasing fluctuation. But μαθηματικὰ represent measurement and definiteness, and are of a totally different nature.

Thirdly, mathematics have always held an exceedingly high place in Plato's esteem, their objects being ἀεὶ ὄντα, and akin to the ideas. It is inconceivable that he should here degrade μαθηματικὰ to the level of phenomena, and say that they are merely, like them, μιμήματα τῶν ἀεὶ ὄντων[2].

The reason why these εἰσιόντα καὶ ἐξιόντα have been taken for μαθηματικὰ is apparently that they have been confused with the μορφαὶ and σχήματα which occur in the simile of the gold, which is employed as an illustration. In the simile the shapes impressed on the gold are the counterpart of the εἰσιόντα καὶ ἐξιόντα, because the gold has to correlate with the substrate; but since the substrate has to be devoid, not only of shape, but quality of every kind, it is impossible to conclude that shapes alone are supposed to enter, and vanish from, the ὑποδοχή. Plato certainly does not say so; he calls the ὑποδοχὴ ἡ τὰ πάντα δεχομένη σώματα φύσις, and the σώματα that come and go are generally

1 56 D.   2 50 C.

styled τὰ εἰσιόντα καὶ ἐξιόντα. The use of ἰδέα and εἶδος occasionally at 50 D, E, and 51 A, need not be taken to imply that shape alone is intended, since the language here is particularly affected by the simile of the gold previously referred to, and form is for the nonce regarded as the typical attribute of body. The simile of the unguents[1], to produce which varied scents are imparted to a scentless fluid, apparently serves Plato's purpose just as well as that of the gold. Shape, consequently, is not the essential point in the simile; if any further proof were wanted, the final moral of the passage at 51 A should suffice : διὸ δὴ τὴν τοῦ γεγονότος ὁρατοῦ καὶ πάντως αἰσθητοῦ μητέρα καὶ ὑποδοχὴν μήτε γῆν μήτε ἀέρα μήτε πῦρ μήτε ὕδωρ λέγωμεν, μήτε ὅσα ἐκ τούτων, μήτε ἐξ ὧν ταῦτα γέγονεν (i.e. the qualities of the Philebus). That is, the εἰσιόντα καὶ ἐξιόντα of the ὑποδοχή, as opposed to those of the gold, are visible air, earth, fire, water, and their constituents and compounds, not μαθηματικὰ at all.

Looking backward over the road that we have travelled since a theory of knowledge was first stated in the Republic, we find that Plato has done much to justify the hope which he there set before us. The dialectician was to start from the world of sensible objects, and, through the continuous assumption of immutable εἴδη, rise to the highest idea of all, an ἀρχὴ ἀνυπόθετος. In the interval he has concluded that many things of which he then posited εἴδη are but instruments to help us along the road to knowledge; they can never serve as its end and goal. Antithetical qualities, for instance, are but the terminology of the senses. The Good and

[1] 50 E.

Beautiful are, generally speaking, the leading predicates of the science of aesthetics. The categories of Same and Other are not ideas, though they are of the utmost importance to the operations of νοῦς and αἴσθησις alike. They are the basis of all classification, and through them alone can we hope to climb the ladder of knowledge at all. They are the foundation of the mathematical sciences, which lead us to the very forecourt of the ἀγαθόν, and which, in default of the ἀγαθὸν itself, furnish us with intermediate εἴδη. He who would make the ascent to the supreme idea must, there-fore, begin with the scientific classification of the objects of sense, through which such information and intellectual power may be acquired as to enable him to posit the existence of mathematical ideas, hypotheses whose truth can only be assured when they have found confirmation in the ἀρχὴ ἀνυπόθετος. Having attained to them he already has an ideal explanation of phenomena, and by diligent study he may hope to imitate in ever-growing perfection the motions of the ἀληθινὸς καὶ θεῖος νοῦς, and realise in some degree the end and aim of being, the ἀγαθόν, ὃ δὴ διώκει μὲν ἅπασα ψυχὴ καὶ τούτου ἕνεκα πάντα πράττει, ἀπομαντευομένη τι εἶναι, ἀποροῦσα δὲ καὶ οὐκ ἔχουσα λαβεῖν ἱκανῶς τί ποτ᾽ ἐστὶν οὐδὲ πίστει χρήσασθαι μονίμῳ, οἷα καὶ περὶ τἆλλα, διὰ τοῦτο δὲ ἀποτυγχάνει καὶ τῶν ἄλλων, εἴ τι ὄφελος ἦν. (Rep. 505 E.)

ESSAY V.

THE PYTHAGOREAN 'Αριθμοὶ AND THEIR RELATION
TO THE PLATONIC IDEAS.

THE subject of Plato's indebtedness to Pythagorean philosophy is one which most authorities agree to disregard and minimise as far as they consistently can. This is due partly to the fact that the mists of neo-Platonism and neo-Pythagoreanism, creeping in between Plato and ourselves, have so obscured the original outlines of the two schools that it seems well-nigh impossible to discover where Pythagoreanism ends and Platonism begins, and partly to the difficulty one always experiences in trying to elicit from Aristotle, our only accredited witness, any unbiassed account of previous schools of thought. The whole question, in fact, is one that calls for the exercise of the critical faculty rather than the laborious collection of evidence. In the present paper, therefore, I do not intend to investigate and catalogue the latent resemblances between the two schools so much as to indicate the great advance which was made by the theory we were last considering upon the early fancies of the Pythagoreans. My first task will be to try to come to some definite conclusions as to what the Pythagoreans really held; my second to compare their views with the

mature doctrine of ἀριθμοὶ which Plato had reached in
the latter half of the *Timaeus*.

The evidence for the genuine beliefs of the Pythagoreans is perforce restricted to that afforded by
Aristotle in various parts of his *Metaphysics*. All other
writers, such as Strabo, Stobaeus, and Alexander
Aphrodisiensis, who give details concerning their
doctrines, lived at too late a date to escape the con-
tamination of the neo-Pythagorean craze of the first
century B. C. Confining ourselves then to Aristotle, let
us set down the substance of the Pythagorean doctrine
as stated in c. v. of *Metaphysics* A and elsewhere.
From the earliest times, we learn, the Pythagoreans
were expert mathematicians, and their chief, and,
perhaps, earliest, dogma was that all things are number.
To quote the account in *Metaphysics* N [1] : " The Pythagoreans, because they perceived many of the attributes
of number to inhere in visible bodies, held that existing
things were numbers ; and these numbers were not
separate from, but immanent in, things. And why ?
Because numerical relations are inherent in harmony,
and in the heavens, and in many other things.' We
gather, then, that Pythagoras and the Pythagoreans
were impressed by the potency and utility of number,
in the first instance, through their mathematical and
musical experiments. In music, Pythagoras himself
had tested its value by his discovery of the chief
intervals of the scale [2] : the quality of different notes was
found to depend upon the proportionate lengths of the
monochord which was struck to produce them. Philolaus,
their great astronomer, had made plain the intricate

[1] *Met.* N. 3. 1090 ᵃ 20.   [2] Cf. Diog. Laert. viii. 12.

harmony and regularity with which the heavenly bodies performed their courses.   It was borne in upon them in general that the numerical properties of a thing were its essential attributes, the most definite account that could be given of it.   Consequently they were led to affirm boldly that things are number, and that the opposite characteristics that appertain to things are but varieties of the ultimate opposition of odd and even. We are told in *Metaphysics* A, c. v., that some Pythagoreans, notably Alcmaeon of Croton, resolved number into two constituents, the odd and the even, or, in geometrical terms, the finite and the infinite, and declared that these constituents, under a variety of names, were the constituents of all existing things. Alcmaeon was so interested in this point that he drew up a lengthy table of the most striking oppositions of this kind; and the antithesis in the first column was invariably regarded as the source of good, that in the second as the origin of evil, in the things which it helped to constitute.

But what was their precise meaning when they said all things are number ? Aristotle tells us plainly enough that they regarded numbers as the material cause of things[1], and that the numbers, instead of being χωριστά, were actually immanent in the things themselves ; nay, the things *were* number. He thereupon proceeds, in c. viii.[2], to draw a ludicrous picture of the Pythagorean universe, in which the absurdity of the theory is made manifest. The Pythagoreans, he says, made the whole universe to consist of number, and it was primarily the heavens, the heavenly bodies, and all the inferior objects

[1] A. 6. 987 ^{b} 27.   [2] A. 8. 990 ^{a} 19.

of perception, that they sought to explain by an elaborate use of their ἀρχαί. Even thus far one can scarcely follow them, seeing that they leave motion entirely unexplained ; but what are we to think, says Aristotle, when they extend their theory even to things that are higher in the category of reality than visible objects, to abstract conceptions, to δόξα, καιρός, ἀδικία, κρίσις or μῖξις ? For they have shown conclusively that each of these, too, is a number. How can we accept this, knowing that there is only one kind of number, that of which external nature is composed? One would expect to find at least two different classes of ἀριθμοί, one appropriate to visible objects, and another to be reserved for νοητά. Are we to imagine a universe in which are to be found, not only the numbers of all αἰσθητά, but the numbers of all νοητὰ too? Dire overcrowding would be the result; yet they cannot surely refuse to admit into their world the number of δόξα, when they say that all numbers alike have μέγεθος, and are inseparable from the world of sense.

This criticism unmistakeably breathes the Aristotelian spirit. One instinctively feels that the writer is not only captious, but biassed by his scientific point of view, and that one may be reading a mere travesty of Pythagorean ideas. One has only to recall the materialistic account of the ψυχογονία of the *Timaeus*[1] to realise that the most philosophical conceptions may at times be set down by Aristotle as sheer materialism. It is, therefore, imperative to examine Aristotle's statements regarding the Pythagoreans thoroughly before accepting them as an authentic account of the facts.

[1] *De An.* A. 2. 404 ᵇ 16.

First of all, he classes the Pythagoreans with the
Ionian nature-philosophers as seeking for reality in
αἰσθητὰ rather than in νοητά, and then immediately
taxes them with inconsistency in admitting νοητὰ into
the sphere of their studies, and accounting for them on
the same principle as αἰσθητά. Now if the Pythagoreans tried to account for νοητὰ and αἰσθητὰ alike, it
is at once obvious that Aristotle has little or no justification for classing them with the nature-philosophers of
Ionia, who concerned themselves with αἰσθητὰ alone.
Quite apart from the question whether their explanation
of things sensible and spiritual was reasonable or not,
the mere circumstance that they took account of
spiritual phenomena is sufficient to separate them from
the early Ionians, and in all probability Aristotle is doing
them an injustice in criticising them as if they looked
at things from the same point of view as these.   The
fact that Aristotle at the beginning[1] cites as typical
examples of their ἀριθμοὶ the numbers of δικαιοσύνη,
καιρός, and νοῦς, and never instances numbers of sensible
things, shows that spiritual phenomena were no mere
appendage in their system; they cannot have been
introduced, as some think, as "a mere sport of the
analogical fancy[2]."   In fact, I regard this two-fold
application of the Pythagorean numbers as the fundamental objection to any view which makes them in any
sense a materialistic system.

The opposite theory, however, is so strongly maintained by Prof. Burnet in his *Early Greek Philosophy*
that it would be as well to consider for a moment the

[1] *Met.* A. 5. 985 ᵇ 29.
[2] See Burnet, *Early Greek Philosophy*, p. 317.

arguments by which he supports it. His opinion is based mainly on the belief that the Pythagoreans were the originators of the doctrine that the point is identical with the monad or unit, that the line, being the first increase of the point, is duality, that the surface is the increase of duality to the number three, and so on. Thus, by identifying the point with the Pythagorean monad, which, according to Aristotle [1], had μέγεθος, and regarding the line as the material increase of this to two units, Prof. Burnet thinks a reasonable origin may be found for Aristotle's statement that the Pythagoreans made number the material cause of things. But surely, if a point be regarded as having μέγεθος, it is to all intents and purposes not a point, but a solid body, and the three increases from point to line, from line to surface, and from surface to solid, are no longer necessary to produce a three-dimensional body. Therefore, although it is possible that the Pythagoreans [2] had not yet reached an *abstract* conception of the point, the line, or the surface, I cannot agree that they held the view indicated by Prof. Burnet. On the contrary, the resolution of the point into the monad, and of the line into duality, would naturally belong to a period in which the science of geometry had been subjected to speculative analysis; and this period could hardly have been that of the Pythagoreans, seeing that Aristotle himself agrees that they were entirely unversed in logic [3], or dialectic, in any degree. It is far more likely that the view in question arose in the time of Plato [4], or that of his immediate predecessors.

[1] See *Met.* M. 6. 1080 [b] 20, 32 ; M. 8. 1083 [b] 13.

[2] See R. and P. 105 A.

[3] *Met.* A. 6. 987 [b] 32.   [4] Cf. *Rep.* 528 A sqq. ; *Laws* 894 A.

Moreover, when one comes to examine the evidence
for this so-called spatial character of the Pythagorean
theory, it is found to consist entirely of Aristotelian
references which either do not apply conclusively to the
Pythagoreans, or are to be discounted either because of
Aristotle's materialistic bias, or for other reasons. The
references in which Aristotle[1] is supposed to say that
the Pythagoreans identified the line with duality
cannot by any stretch of language be proved to point to
the Pythagoreans; on the contrary, the text seems to
indicate that the later Platonists alone can be intended,
and the same criticism applies to the passages[2] in which
the Pythagoreans are supposed to make the monad and
the point identical. As for the statement that the
monad or unit, according to the Pythagoreans[3], had
μέγεθος, here Aristotle is simply telling his old story
over again, and representing the Pythagorean number
as a material basis, without inspiring any additional
confidence in his view, or taking account of the fundamental objection which was mentioned before. The
passages in Aristotle's *Physics*[4], in which the Pythagorean void is identified with the ἄπειρον, prove nothing,
since the term ἄπειρον might quite well be applied to
the void without indicating necessarily that the ἄπειρον
is inevitably a *res extensa*, or that number, of which it
is sometimes a στοιχεῖον, is invariably, or originally,
spatial. The reference to Eurytus[5], in which the latter
is said to have tried to arrive at the numbers of man,

---

[1] *Met.* Z. 11. 1036ᵇ 12. Cf. *de An.* iii. c. 4. 429ᵇ 20; *de Caelo* A.
1. 268ᵃ 7.

[2] *Met.* Z. 2. 1028ᵇ 16.   [3] See p. 93.

[4] *Phys.* Γ. 4. 203ᵃ 7; Δ. 6. 213ᵇ 23.

[5] *Met.* N. 5. 1092ᵇ 10. Cf. M. 8. 1083ᵇ 18.

horse, etc., by sketching their outlines, and counting the number of pebbles required to produce them, comes nearest to supporting Prof. Burnet's theory. In isolation, however, it cannot be said to carry conviction, since, in the first place, the process described is extremely obscure, and it is hard to say exactly what Eurytus was aiming at, and, secondly, one can quite well imagine the Pythagoreans using childish methods of this kind to arrive at the numbers of concrete things, without asserting that their whole theory arose in this way. The particular method ascribed to Eurytus was very likely only one of the ways which the younger Pythagoreans employed to give the master's theory a universal application. I cannot, therefore, regard any of this evidence as conclusive in proving that the number-doctrine had a spatial or geometrical origin.

It will appear that little or no satisfaction is to be had by regarding the Pythagorean philosophy through the eyes of later schools. A truer insight, it seems to me, may be gained if we go back in thought to a period anterior to that of Pythagoras himself, and endeavour for a moment to view him rather as the heir of Egyptian and Babylonian mysticism[1], than as the forerunner of Plato. Here, of course, one is approaching a field of research which is as yet only beginning to yield definite results, and from which a rich harvest may be expected in the future. Sufficient evidence, however, is to be

---

[1] I am of course using "mysticism" here in the sense in which it is most applicable to Eastern beliefs, as the association of divinity with certain material symbols for purely fanciful reasons, quite apart from any intellectual process. (See Inge, *Christian Mysticism*, Appendix B.)

found in hieroglyphic and hieratic literature [1] to make it practically certain that the Egyptians in ancient times attributed not merely to numbers but to the spoken word in general a curious and mysterious potency which is wholly foreign to western nations.   In the Pyramid Texts, in fact, we find mentioned a god called Khern, i.e. "Word" (compare λόγος).   That which to us is simply an instrument of expression, created by man to serve the necessities of human intercourse, was regarded by them as belonging to an independent order of existence with a vitality of its own, and endowed with all the attributes that compose the description of a living thing. The "word" had a personality like that of a human being[2], and, provided it were pronounced in the proper manner, and in the proper tone of voice, was powerful in the service of him by whom it was uttered.   The creation of the world was due to the interpretation in words by Thoth of the will of the deity.

Number especially seems to have been invested by the Egyptians with these peculiar powers.   By the four-fold repetition of their curse-formula, under proper conditions[3], the speedy realisation of their desires was ensured.   This potency of four is connected by some with the gods of the four points of the compass, but it may have a far less obvious explanation.   Their all-powerful and beneficent deities were classed mainly in groups of odd numbers[4], especially of nine and seven, and, of course, the famous three.   This preference for odd numbers in

---

[1] See Dr Budge, *Egyptian Magic*, preface, pp. x., xi.
[2] See Dr Budge, translation of *Book of the Dead*, p. 147.
[3] Dr Budge, *Egyptian Religion*, p. 107.
[4] Dr Budge, *Egyptian Religion*, pp. 89–91.

representing divinity seems to indicate that the odd numbers had with them, as with the Pythagoreans after them, a pre-eminence over the even as being a power for good. Seven also played an important part in their rites and ceremonies. The Book of the Dead tells of the seven Ārits or halls[1] in each of which three gods were seated, guarded by seven doorkeepers, seven watchers, and seven heralds, and of the seventh formula which, when recited, procured entrance at the door of any one of the seven mansions of Osiris.

The Babylonians, too, apparently, gave special prominence to number; like the Pythagoreans they realised its value in the practical sciences of calculation, and they also regarded it as of mystical significance. There is evidence to prove[2] that their multiplication table was remarkably well-developed, that they counted up to 12,960,000, and that their tables of weights and measures were very far advanced. Their measurements of time seem to have been based on the division of the zodiac into twelve parts[3]: thus the Babylonian day was made to consist of twelve double-hours, as the faces of our clocks still indicate. That they assigned magical properties to number and preferred one number over another is plain from the fact that they invariably regarded some days as lucky, others (particularly the seventh) as unlucky. The importance of the number seven, not only among the Babylonians, but with the Eastern nations generally, is of course abundantly

---

[1] *Egyptian Magic*, p. 165.

[2] See Hilprecht, *The Nippur Expedition*, pp. 28 ff.

[3] Cf. Winckler, *Die Weltanschauung des Alten Orients* (Leipzig, 1903).

illustrated in the Old Testament writings—in the seven towers of Babel, and the numerous repetitions of seven in the instructions regarding Jewish ritual (e.g. Leviticus 4. 6; 14. 16, 51; Numbers 23; Ezek. 40. 22).

Now, although the evidence which has as yet come to light is but slight, it is at least clear that the Egyptians and Babylonians assigned to number a great importance, and attached to it the functions of an independent agency in a fashion that appears strange to western minds. They regarded it as something endued with power to heal or to harm, to create or to destroy, according as its nature, being good or bad, prompted. Like the "word," it could be described by attributes, favourable or unfavourable, such as were applied to human agents themselves. If this, then, was the general attitude of the East towards number in ancient times, if it was regarded almost with the awe and reverence due to Deity itself, it would be little wonder that there should arise a school, peculiarly subject to Oriental influence, whose leading tenet was that number is the sole arbiter of life. There is no need to prove that Pythagoras ever had actual dealings with Egypt, Babylon, or any other Eastern country; it is undeniable that his system was chiefly a farrago of religious and mathematical precepts, which are analogous to Eastern, rather than Hellenic, thought.

The remarkable importance assigned by the Egyptians to the more general "word" seems to have borne fruit at a later time, and to have led, directly or indirectly, to a form of the Heracleitean philosophy which gave to words and names a permanence which was denied to the visible things of the universe. The Heracleitean Cratylus[1], who thus saw in ὀνόματα the inmost reality of the fluctuating objects of sense, could not conceivably be termed a materialist. Why then should Pythagoras, the heir of Egyptian and Babylonian mysticism, be accused of materialism for declaring that numbers, to which the learned people of the East had always attributed the greatest magical significance, are the truest reality of things, that things are really number? An assertion of this sort did not necessitate any art of διαλεκτική, which we know Pythagoras lacked; to make it there was needed only the impetuous logic of the religious enthusiast, which Pythagoras certainly was. The induction which he drew was neither that of the physicist, nor of the philosopher, but that of the mystic.

My contention, therefore, is that the Pythagorean doctrine described by Aristotle is far more reasonably regarded as the natural development of a mystical view of numbers than as a truly philosophical or physical system. Aristotle, impatient as he was of everything pertaining to the occult, might quite well describe such a system in the obscure and self-contradictory language which we have noted. The point upon which he insists throughout is that the Pythagorean numbers were not abstract conceptions (χωριστά), like those of Plato. The Pythagoreans had not, in fact, advanced sufficiently in scientific speculation to make the abstract calculations of our own time: when they counted it was always apparently with a reference to external objects of one kind or another. Aristotle, therefore, concludes that

---

[1] See Plato, *Cratylus* 386 D, E ; 390 D, E.

their doctrine that things are number can only mean
that number was to them a material cause, and that
each unit had a μέγεθος which contributed to the bulk
of the thing. But if the alternative offered us by
Aristotle is such a *reductio ad absurdum*, surely he has
misunderstood the point at issue. The Pythagoreans
certainly did not conceive of number abstractly, but
might they not have regarded it vaguely as the
mystical cause of things, and have allowed their
statements to vacillate, after the manner of mystics,
between assertions that things are reflexions of number,
and bolder proclamations that things are number itself?
Aristotle certainly assigns to them both doctrines
indiscriminately[1], without any consciousness that the
two views are mutually destructive. If the Pythagoreans did make use of both forms indifferently (and we
have no reason to doubt it), then Aristotle is assuredly
mistaken in classing them as materialists. By far the
more natural supposition is that their vague and
mystical modes of expression were to him incompre-
hensible, and the simplest solution for him was to set
them down as materialists, although on this hypothesis
the extension of their doctrine to immaterial things was
a source of constant irritation. The fact that the
symbolical element and the doctrine of μίμησις did
undoubtedly play their part in the Pythagorean
system seems to me to make it almost certain that
the Pythagoreans were mystics rather than philosophers.

    This conclusion appears to me still more likely when
one considers the subordinate clause of Pythagoreanism,

[1] See *Met.* A. 5. 985 b 27; 987 b 11.

viz., that the odd and the even, being the constituents of number, are the constituents of all existing things. Since all existence has its source in the antagonism of opposites, whatever object we may care to consider is to be regarded as a composition of the opposing forces of odd and even. Now here we have the popular notion of the contradictions of life, which recurs in Heracleitus' γένεσις ἐξ ἐναντίων, brought into line with the empirical division of number into odd and even. There are two sides, said Alcmaeon, to most things in life; there is the finite and the infinite, good and evil, male and female, right and left, rest and motion. Number, too, the essence of things, has two phases, the odd and the even; hence it must be that the antitheses of existing things are but variant forms of the ultimate antithesis of odd and even. But this odd and even are also said by Aristotle[1] to have been regarded by the Pythagoreans as material elements. This view seems at first sight to be even harder to justify than the preceding; yet the explanation becomes perfectly easy when once we suppose Aristotle to be understanding mystical and semi-religious formulae in a literal sense. Number once exalted as the mystical basis of things, nothing is more natural than that its fundamental division into odd and even should be regarded as the mystical origin of all the multitudinous antitheses of existing things. If number works good or ill according as it be lucky or unlucky, odd or even, and if number is, somehow, the reality of things themselves, then assuredly the good

[1] e.g. *Met.* N. 3. 1091 ᵃ 15.

qualities of things must be caused by oddness, the bad qualities by evenness, in number.

Finally, if one views the Pythagoreans as mystics rather than philosophers, one has no difficulty in the fact that their scheme took account of immaterial, as well as material, phenomena. The mystic is not concerned to make distinctions of this sort. The smaller the barrier set up between spiritual and material the better for his purpose. A theory that is based on fancy and dogma does not need to be tested by philosophical distinctions.

Before passing on to the consideration of Plato, we have to note that although the original idea of Pythagoreanism probably had its source in the Orient, the members of the school apparently worked it out in detail according to their own methods, relying chiefly on superficial analogies. "The Pythagoreans," says Aristotle at A. 5. 985 ᵇ 27, "believed that they detected in numbers certain resemblances (ὁμοιώματα) to existing and phenomenal things," and immediately afterwards: "Phenomena indeed appeared to them to be copied from (ἀφωμοιῶσθαι) numbers." The reasons given by later commentators for their choice of particular numbers for particular things are fanciful enough. Some of them may also, as Aristotle indicates, have had recourse to the absurd tactics of Eurytus in order to arrive at the numbers of material objects. These details are of slight importance; they only go to show that the school soon lost what serious scientific interest it had possessed. The main result of our enquiry is that the Pythagoreans were not in the strict sense philosophers, that they upheld number, in a vague and mystical way, as the source from which all things proceeded, and that the obscure and indefinite form of their statements, and the indiscriminate application of their theory to material and spiritual things alike, show that they had not any exact knowledge of the nature either of number or of form.

Our next task is to compare this doctrine with the numbers of Plato, and to estimate the difference between them. That Plato was steeped in Pythagorean fancy, and extremely familiar with Pythagorean teaching, cannot be doubted by those who are acquainted with his dialogues. Their cardinal doctrines of the transmigration of souls, and of the destruction and reconstruction of the world in definite periods, appear again and again in his works. He is constantly referring to them and adducing them as authorities on matters that appertain to mathematics. That a great gulf, however, yawned between their system and his cannot but appear when one recalls the highly developed mathematical theory that was put forward in the last part of the *Timaeus*. There we found Plato[1] making a new beginning, and pitching his song in a different key. The greatest part of his message, perhaps, had already been delivered; he had proclaimed his belief in a universal mind that is the ultimate source of all phenomena. The ἀγαθόν, which in the *Republic* represented the goal and aim for which the whole creation strives, has resolved itself into a θεῖος καὶ ἀληθινὸς νοῦς, and the divine ideas, which have held his imagination captive so long, are but certain aspects and determinations of that Reason.

[1] *Tim.* c. xvii. p. 47 E.

But the ἀγαθόν, with Plato, was not to be a mere
hypothesis; it was to be known and realised; it
was the goal of all knowledge. How then is he to
attain to it? How is he to prepare himself to come
into relations with the παράδειγμα of all existence?
He can only begin, as the *Republic* suggested long
before, with the world of phenomena around him,
the world which he perceives through αἴσθησις—that
perverted mode of apprehension which belongs to the
animal kind alone, and which is the inevitable consequence of the deliberate degeneration of souls, and
their transmigration through endless ages into ever-
varying forms of life. Starting, then, with the world
of sense, Plato endeavours to rise from the perception
of body to an intermediate class of ideas which will
serve as objects of knowledge until the supreme νοῦς is
within reach. In order to describe these ideas, he is
forced to delineate an entirely new conception, that of
abstract space, the ὑποδοχὴ γενέσεως, within which he
builds up mentally the things of time and space,
conceived in terms of their geometrical construction.
He shows us that all the perceptible objects of the
world around us are only perceived subject to conditions of geometrical relation[1], and that the exact
expression of these varying relations is the highest
mental interpretation of the things they denote.
The mind translates into its own terms the materials
of sense, and when this happens we are journeying
from the material towards the ideal. All the phenomena of nature, therefore, may on this view be
regarded as copies of a mathematical idea, according

[1] Cf. *Laws* 894 A.

to which a certain ἀριθμός of primary triangular forms
is supposed to constitute the characteristic εἶδος or
shape of the particular thing.

Now the first and obvious distinction to be drawn
between Plato and the Pythagoreans is that the former
considered number, form, and space, too, in the abstract
and not in the concrete. Number, he tells us in the
Parmenides[1], is generated as soon as any notion, of
whatever kind, comes before the mind for consideration.
The mind is forced to count, as soon as it begins to be
active. Number is, consequently, of a subjective nature
only ; it cannot have an independent existence apart
from the thinking mind. As to form, we know that he
had always in his mind's eye the ideal triangle and the
ideal pyramid of γεωμετρία, which, although they had
been conceived of course before Plato's day, were almost
certainly unknown to the Pythagoreans, whatever later
writers, such as Proclos, may say to the contrary. There
is, at all events, no sure or conclusive evidence that they
had advanced to a conception of abstract geometrical
forms. As for the conception of pure, abstract space,
it is extremely doubtful whether any of Plato's predecessors had attained to such a clear or complete notion
of it as that which we find in the *Timaeus*.

Once Plato had reached these highly abstract
conceptions, he could indeed reconstruct the world
mathematically without any fear of the ridicule that
attended the attempts of the Pythagoreans. Anyone
that allowed the truth and reality of mental conceptions would, under these conditions, permit him
to have ἀριθμοί and yet be sane. It may be objected

[1] *Parm.* 143 D, E.

that something of the mystical element remains in the
hope, vague though it be, that he may some day be
enabled, through a diligent pursuit of the ἀριθμοί, to
rise to the knowledge of the supreme reality itself.
Such an aspiration may perhaps be termed mystical,
in so far as it makes an assertion without affording
visible or reasonable justification, but if it be mysticism
at all, it is the mysticism[1] of the man who thinks, the
man who realises and does not confound, as the Pythagoreans did, the means and the end. 'Aριθμοὶ to him
are only a stepping-stone. While pursuing them he
never loses sight of the great reality beyond, which a
man must seek κτήσεως ἕνεκα εὐδαίμονος βίου.

Let us endeavour, then, to sum up the difference
between the Pythagorean theory and that of Plato.
Plato inherited from the Pythagorean school the doctrine
that the real essence of a thing is not material air,
earth or water, as the case might be, but a certain
number, of which the thing was, in some mysterious
and inexplicable way, a likeness. The only reason
which the authors of the doctrine could give for their
assumption was the fact that they had fancied certain
resemblances to exist between number and things, and
that they had, moreover, been astonished at its efficacy
in their musical and mathematical experiments. They
could assign no reasonable basis for their faith; they
were more mystics than metaphysicians. Plato, pursuing diligently the study of mathematics, came to

---

[1] Mysticism in this sense would be identical with Inge's conception
of it in his *Christian Mysticism*—the "formless speculation" which
comes to the aid of philosophy against materialism and scepticism.
(See *Christian Mysticism*, Lect. i. p. 22.)

the same general conclusion, namely, that number plays a great part in our experience of phenomena. It would have been unnatural for him, however, to rest content with this vague generalisation. The severe discipline to which he subjected himself in the *Parmenides*, the *Sophist*, and kindred dialogues, had made clear to him the nature of mind and its mode of operation. Sensation, with him, was a degenerate form of apprehension, arising from the body, with which the soul is clogged. It can *never* give accurate information concerning the universe. Sensation told him that the universe is bodily; whereas his reason knew that its truest and highest nature was that of mind and soul. The philosopher must, however, *begin* with the data of sensation, for thence he may, by the activity of pure νοῦς, discover the conditions and principles which underlie the ever-varying illusion of sense. Geometry comes to his aid first, and teaches him the ultimate laws of bulk and surface; then, by the help of pure arithmetic, he is enabled to express in the language of the intellect the entire sensible world. And this, he feels, is not mere imagination; he is approaching the truth of things. For the universe, after all, is real, and it is the only object of knowledge; only it is not just what our senses perceive. Therefore the more intellectual our account of it becomes, the nearer we are to knowing it as it really is. And the individual soul is a copy of the universal παράδειγμα, the θεῖος νοῦς, though the resemblance is for the present obscured through the adverse power of sin. It must inevitably, some day, return to its first estate, if only it cultivates diligently the activities of reason

that have been planted within it, and models its life
upon that of the great Soul of the universe.

Such a view is surely not unworthy of the greatest
philosopher of antiquity. The mathematical ideas,
with him, did not, as with the Pythagoreans, represent
the final analysis of the universe. They were μεταξύ
τι, an intermediate stage merely, to prepare the soul
for the comprehension of the supreme παράδειγμα.
Let us not set down to him the absurd accretions which
were superimposed upon him by his feeble and literal-
minded followers, who, engrossed with the thought
of ideal numbers to the exclusion of all else, confused
their master's doctrine hopelessly with that of his
Pythagorean predecessors, thereby casting an un-
merited cloud upon the brilliancy of his philosophical
reputation. For the Pythagoreans were children,
playing with pebbles upon the shore of the vast ocean
of knowledge; but Plato had already embarked, with
his sails full-set for the open sea.

ESSAY VI.

THE ARISTOTELIAN CRITIQUE OF THE IDEAS AND NUMBERS OF PLATO.

ANY account of the Platonic system, particularly in its maturer form, would be imperfect without some reference to the *Metaphysics* of Aristotle; for in them is to be found the only contemporary evidence extant respecting the nature of Plato's doctrine at a time when he himself had ceased to commit his thoughts to writing. To ignore them entirely would, indeed, be a serious error, when one considers that a man's published work is not always the most accurate representation of his mature conclusions, but that his ultimate views are often reserved for the inner circle of friends or pupils, who may, if they will, record them after his death. Objection is frequently made to the testimony of Aristotle in this connexion on the ground of his personal antipathy to the idealist point of view, and the consequent unfairness, not only of his criticism, but of his statement, of Plato's teaching. This, however, is not sufficient reason to deter us from interrogating Aristotle as far as we can, provided we assess his evidence at our own valuation. When all

due allowance is made for the philosophical bias of
the witness, there will surely remain a residuum of
information which will contribute something to the
discovery of the true state of affairs. Therefore, since
our aim is to come to some conclusions regarding the
Platonic system itself, our endeavour will be to review
the information with which Aristotle supplies us, rather
than to attempt any estimate of his critical ability,
although the character of his criticisms must necessarily
reveal itself, to some extent, in the course of our examination; also, for the sake of clearness and convenience,
his account of the Platonic system in general should
claim our attention before the detailed exposition of
the numbers in Books M and N, and in other isolated
passages.

Following Aristotle's frequent statement[1], then, we
find that the ideal theory, as originally conceived,
before it became connected with the nature of numbers,
was promulgated as a complementary article to the
Heracleitean doctrine of flux. Its supporters were
convinced that if there was to be ἐπιστήμη or φρόνησις
of any kind, there must be existences, other than ῥέοντα,
endued with the permanency in which these were
lacking; and whereas Socrates, intent on morality and
ethics, was content to seek this knowledge in the definitions of general notions merely, which definitions were
obtained through ῥέοντα, Plato and his followers posited
certain permanent existences separate from ῥέοντα
(χωριστά), which they termed ideas, and of which, as
distinguished from ῥέοντα, the definition was given.
The consequence was that they supposed ideas to exist

[1] *Met.* A. 6. 987 ᵃ 29 seq.; *Met.* M. 4. 1078 ᵇ 9; 9. 1086 ᵃ 35.

of every general predicate, after the fashion of a man
who, in making a calculation, believes it easier to count a
larger number than a smaller one; and the relation which
obtained between these ideas and ῥέοντα they termed
μέθεξις[1]. These, of course, are the ideas as described in
the *Republic* and *Phaedo*, where they are assumed for
the express purpose of clearing up the mystery of predication, and they meet with the same objection (that
of the τρίτος ἄνθρωπος) from Aristotle that Plato himself urges against them in the *Parmenides*. But, apart
from that, Aristotle continues, the doctrine is very
unsatisfactory, because, in the first place, the arguments used by the Idealists do not carry conviction,
and, in the second, their contentions result in our
having ideas of things for which we do not recognise
ideas. The latter criticism is justified by references to
dialogues in which are given the accounts that conflict
with the orthodox system. Thus, if one accepts their
arguments regarding the sciences, there will be an idea
for every science (cf. *Rep.* 476 E); according to their
explanation of the ἓν ἐπὶ πολλῶν, there will be an idea
for all negations (*Rep.* 596 A); also, in virtue of the
possibility of νόησις concerning things dead, we must
accept ideas of φθαρτά (*Parm.* 132 B, C). But orthodox
Platonists apparently do not have ideas of these things.
Moreover, the most accurate expositions postulate ideas
of relations[2], of which we present-day Platonists refuse
to admit ideas, and in another case the τρίτος ἄνθρωπος[3]
argument itself is brought against the ideal theory.
Another inconsistency is found in the fact that, whereas

---

[1] *Met.* A. 6. 987 ᵇ 9.
[2] *Phaedo* 74 A.   [3] *Parm.* 132 A.

the Platonic teaching makes the ideas responsible for γένεσις of any kind, there is γένεσις of some things, such as δακτύλιος and οἰκία[1], of which the Platonists say there are no ideas. The Plato whom Aristotle knew apparently claimed ideas of natural objects only, such as πῦρ, σάρξ, κεφαλή (διὸ δὴ οὐ κακῶς ὁ Πλάτων ἔφη[2] ὅτι εἴδη ἐστὶν ὁπόσα φύσει, εἴπερ ἔστιν εἴδη...οἷον πῦρ, σάρξ, κεφαλή), and these ideas were pre-eminently of a numerical nature, composed of the same στοιχεῖα[3] as visible things, viz., the ἓν and the ἀόριστος δυάς, or, τὸ μέγα καὶ τὸ μικρόν. Hence the absurdity of those accounts which posit ideas of a multitude of things, for, according to these, number, and not the dyad, is first in importance, and the darling theory of the Platonists is overthrown.

Such, in brief, is the substance of the rambling sketch given by Aristotle, and the writer of Books M and N, of the Platonic system in general. Disjointed as it is, however, it furnishes us with several conclusions regarding Aristotle's relation to the Platonic teaching. In the first place, he certainly was not aware of any single harmonious theory in which all the statements in the dialogues, written at different periods in Plato's career, were to be reconciled. On the contrary, the dialogues furnish him with constant occasion for discontent; they contradict one another, and militate for the most part against the received Platonism of the day. Aristotle, therefore, did not hold, with certain modern critics, that the ideal theory was a single conception that remained essentially the same throughout.

[1] *Met.* M. 5. 1080 ᵃ 5.   [2] *Met.* Λ. 3. 1070 ᵃ 18.
[3] *Met.* A. 6. 988 ᵃ 11.

Secondly, he speaks as one who has read the dialogues
for himself, as a self-imposed task, without any
illuminating aid from the one who wrote them. They
are a problem which he does not seem able to solve.
Clearly, then, Aristotle could not at any time have had
the advantage of hearing Plato himself lecture on the
subject of the dialogues; he could not have known
the ideal theory at first hand during its various
developments. By the time he came to the Academy
the theory must have suffered material alteration, and
apparently no great pains were taken to make the later
phase consonant with the former. All Plato's strictly
philosophical dialogues were probably already written,
and his work lay chiefly in discoursing personally to
his pupils on the subject of the ideas as ἀριθμοί—so
at least one gathers from the numerous references[1]
to the ἄγραφα δόγματα and ἄγραφοι συνουσίαι made
by Aristotle and later writers. At any rate, it is the
ἀριθμοί that loom largest on Aristotle's horizon; the
Platonists of his day devoted themselves to them alone,
and schism even arose in their ranks on account of
their conflicting views regarding them. It is quite
natural, therefore, that Aristotle, being steeped in the
contemporary views of the school, should display considerable ignorance regarding the evolution of Plato's
thought during the interval between the *Phaedo* and
the *Timaeus*, and should fail to realise the value of
that deliberative and corrective process which we have
examined in previous essays. That the ideal theory was
not in the beginning identical with its latest phase, he
assures us; but of the intervening stages he knows

[1] See Ar. *Phys.* Δ. 2. 209 b 15 ; Procl. *in Tim.* p. 205.

nothing.   But, although we may be disposed to regard
him as a dubious authority on the ideal theory at large,
we cannot rob him of his importance as a contemporary
student of Platonism, when we are examining the latest
stage of that theory.

This so-called number-theory, as described by
Aristotle, is so full of difficulty, and the dissensions
among its supporters are of so intricate a nature, that
a complete examination of the evidence is necessary
before one can hope to disentangle the views of Plato
from those of his successors; and for this purpose it
will be wiser to postpone the consideration of the
condensed and confused statements of Book A till we
have weighed the more detailed accounts of Books M
and N.   The author of M and N, writing perhaps more
as a Platonist than as Plato's contemporary, describes at
great length the conflicting tenets of the Platonists of
his day.   There were, apparently, at least three different
sections[1] among the Platonists of that time, one school
postulating the existence of two kinds of numbers, the
ideal and the mathematical, which were widely different,
although alike χωριστά, another affirming that μαθηματικὰ and ἰδέαι are one nature, and that the ἰδέαι find
expression in mathematical terms, and yet a third, who,
according to M. 1086 ᵃ 2 and N. 1090 ᵃ 17, discarded ideas
altogether, and sought refuge in μαθηματικὰ simply,
declaring, like the Pythagoreans, that things are really
numbers.

The first of these theories is a complicated one[2], for
these Platonists believe that the ideal, as opposed to the

---

[1] See M. 1. 1076 ᵃ 16 ff.;   M. 8. 1083 ᵃ 21 ff.;   M. 9. 1086 ᵃ 2 ff.;
N. 3. 1090 ᵇ 16 ff.

[2] See M. 6. 1080 ᵃ 15 ff.

mathematical, numbers, differ one from the other in
quality, and are ἀσύμβλητοι, i.e., no mathematical
operations, either of addition or multiplication, can
take place in regard to them. Whereas mathematical
numbers are formed by the addition of a plurality of
units, all of equal value, the units of ideal numbers are
in each case distinct, and cannot enter into combination
with those of other ideal numbers. This at least seems
to Aristotle the most plausible explanation of the word
ἀσύμβλητος, though he acknowledges that it may be
construed to mean that even the monads of each ideal
number itself, if it has any, are not to be added to one
another, in which case, of course, the ideas of number
will not have the properties of number at all. It is
hard to believe, as Aristotle justly points out, that
there can exist a number which is not to be formed by
the addition or multiplication of units; and, on the
other view of ἀσύμβλητος, it would seem necessary to
make, not only the monads, but the triads, pentads, and
all the other constituents of the numbers, to be
ἀσύμβλητοι as well—a truly complicated task (M. 7.
1082 ᵃ 1 seq.). The first doctrine, then, is characterised
by ideas of number, which are ranked in a qualitative
order (τὸν μὲν ἔχοντα τὸ πρότερον καὶ ὕστερον τὰς
ἰδέας, M. 1080 ᵇ 12), together with mathematical
number, apart from the ideas and αἰσθητά. These
ideas are generally styled πρῶτοι ἀριθμοί[1], in contradistinction to the numbers of the second school,
and are not made to consist, like the ideas of the second
school, of the ἕν and the indefinite dyad (see N. 3. 1090 ᵇ
34: cf. M. 8. 1083 ᵃ 32). Mathematical number, more-

[1] See M. 7. 1081 ᵃ 4, 21.

116   THE ARISTOTELIAN CRITIQUE OF

over, was regarded by them as μεταξὺ τοῦ εἰδητικοῦ καὶ τοῦ αἰσθητοῦ, holding the same position as the μαθηματικὰ of the *Republic*, except that it is now considered to be something between ideal and material *number* exclusively. The old multitude of ideas, representing everything which can be predicated of anything, have dropped into the background, and the ideal numbers are the only ideas, and, in virtue of being ideal numbers, are also the ideas of material things. Such, at least, seems to be the necessary inference from the discussion in M. 8. 1084 [ab], where the αὐτοὶ ἀριθμοί, or ideal, as distinguished from ordinary, numbers, are certainly referred to (1084 [a] 19, 23), and it is implied that each of the αὐτοὶ ἀριθμοὶ stands for the idea of an animal or the like. There it is also hinted that the ideal series ends with the δεκάς, but this is not advanced as a compulsory part of the creed.

Opposed to the Platonists, who posit the two classes of numbers, is the school (least commendable of all, says Aristotle[1]) who say that the ἓν is the ἀρχὴ and στοιχεῖον of all things, and that by its combination with the δυὰς ἀόριστος[2] number is produced. These apparently agree with the former school in making numbers χωριστά, but their numbers are not, like the ideal numbers of the first school, ἀσύμβλητοι. They saw the folly of having two distinct sets of number, and their contention seems to have been[3] that the ideas took the form of numbers, or were expressible in numbers, for they refused to agree with the more Pythagorising section that numbers are in themselves οὐσία[4]. They seemed to justify their position by their speculative analysis,

---

[1] M. 8. 1083 [b] 2.   [2] M. 6. 1080 [b] 6.
[3] M. 9. 1086 [a] 7.   [4] M. 9. 1086 [a] 2; N. 3. 1090 [b] 17.

not only of number, but of all μαθηματικά. After generating number out of the ἕν and the ἀόριστος δυάς, they proceeded to generate μέγεθος out of number and ὕλη, or χώρα[1], in virtue of their resolution of the solid into 4, the surface into 3, the line into 2, and so on. They are also represented[2] as in some instances generating the various aspects of μέγεθος out of varieties of the ἀόριστος δυάς, or τὸ μέγα καὶ τὸ μικρόν, which is the ultimate basis of number and all things.

The third section, who, fearful of the δυσχέρεια[3] that beset the ideas in general, took refuge in μαθηματικὰ alone, seem to have been infected with the taint of Pythagoreanism, though apparently they did not go so far as to make numbers a material cause, as Aristotle would put it (M. 1. 1076ᵃ 35). They did not indulge, like their contemporaries, in the speculative analysis of number into the ἕν and the ἀόριστος δυάς; but they are represented instead as evolving all number from the addition or multiplication of ἕν[4].

Now it is at once obvious that of the three theories the first is by far the most complicated, inasmuch as it is at pains to draw fine distinctions between the εἰδητικοὶ and the μαθηματικοὶ ἀριθμοί, and applies different phraseology to the two kinds. The εἰδητικοὶ ἀριθμοὶ are πρῶτοι ἀριθμοί, and are incapable of mathematical operation of any sort, whereas the μαθηματικὰ are μεταξύ, and are subject to mathematical calculation. The upholders of this view, moreover, did not seem to endorse the theory of number as being compounded of the ἕν and the ἀόριστος δυάς; they seem, in fact, to have left the

[1] N. 3. 1090ᵇ 21.   [2] M. 9. 1085ᵃ 9.   [3] M. 9. 1086ᵃ 3.
[4] M. 8. 1083ᵃ 21.

details of their theory unexplained, not even trying to give an account of the μαθηματικοὶ ἀριθμοί[1]. We may, however, draw several inferences regarding this section of the Platonic school. The fact that μαθηματικά, on this view of the numbers, are almost always termed μεταξύ, has already led Prof. Cook Wilson[2] to infer that the ideas of number referred to here are identical with the earlier doctrine of the *Republic*. While allowing that the discussion of μαθηματικά in Book B, and perhaps a few other passages, may refer to the theory of the *Republic* alone, I believe that the details concerning the ἀσύμβλητοι ἀριθμοὶ in M and N cannot but belong to the late theory of numbers, which, in the hands of one section of Platonism, was contaminated with the mathematical teaching of the *Republic*[3]. There, it will be remembered, there is an eternal and immutable idea of every mathematical notion, besides the abstract conception of which the scientific definition treats. This later school of Platonists, as far as we can judge, took over this portion of the educational scheme of the *Republic*, and, ignoring for the most part the geometrical, astronomical, and other μεταξύ (A. 9. 992ᵇ 13), used it to explain the difference between ideal and mathematical number. The theory of the *Republic*, however, was assuredly pressed into the service of the later number-theory, in order, no doubt, to afford a plausible justification for having idea-numbers at all[4]. The ἀσύμβλητοι ἀριθμοί, since each represented a unique entity, were ἕν, and not πολλά, and were, therefore, not subject to the objection

---

[1] N. 3. 1090ᵇ 34.

[2] See Art. by Prof. Cook Wilson, *Class. Rev.* vol. xviii. p. 247.

[3] *Rep.* 525 A ff.   [4] See M. 7. 1081ᵃ 6 ff.

raised by Aristotle, that if *any* number could be an idea, the ideas for each object would be multitudinous. It is at any rate clear that these Platonists thought their ideal numbers to be the ideas of things. The writer of Book M[1], referring at c. 8 to the πρῶτοι ἀριθμοί, which he shows to be subject to the same absurdities as ordinary ἀριθμοί, gives as hypothetical instances of the numbers that stood for ideas of things ἡ τετρὰς αὐτὴ and ἡ δυὰς αὐτή, thereby showing clearly that the supporters of the πρῶτοι ἀριθμοὶ used them to express the reality of visible things. In common with the rest of the school, they held that number was the highest expression of reality, but it was not mathematical, but ideal, number that was so distinguished.

To this section of the school, undoubtedly, belongs that curious article of belief which Aristotle attributes to the Platonists in the sixth chapter of the first book of his *Ethics*[2]. The later Platonists, he says, did not admit the existence of an idea to correspond to a group of things whose members were in the relation of πρότερον καὶ ὕστερον to one another (i.e., they did not accept the doctrine of the *Republic in toto*, and allow an idea of every predicate), and, consequently, did not recognise a single idea of number to correspond to the group of ideal numbers, which were in the relation of πρότερον καὶ ὕστερον to one another. These Platonists, in short, utilised a part only of the machinery of the ideal theory of the *Republic*. The assumption of an idea for every predicate was for them unnecessary, since the logic of predication, thanks to Plato's dialectical zeal as exemplified

[1] M. 8. 1084ᵃ 23 seq.   [2] *Eth. N.* I. vi. 1096ᵃ 17.

in the *Parmenides,* the *Sophist,* and elsewhere, was not to them a mystery, such as it had been to the Eleatic Zeno and his contemporaries. They retained apparently ideas of numbers only, and these ideas had the pre-eminent virtue of representing the reality of all existing things; and, although they constituted an ideal series, they were to be exempt from the original rule that every group of particulars has an idea corresponding to it.

The second class of Platonists did not feel com-pelled to have recourse to these shifts for main-taining the doctrine of the ideas as numbers. There did not seem to them to be any absurdity in supposing that the ideas should be represented as ordinary ἀριθμοί, and that the highest expression of the reality of the universe was to be found in mathematical formulae. They laid great stress on the derivation of number from the ἕν and the ἀόριστος δυάς, which were the στοιχεῖα, not merely of number, but of all existing things. In fact, it was in virtue of thus containing in their essence the elements to which all existing things must ultimately be reduced, that numbers were marked out by them as the ideal prototypes of things. Of these two στοιχεῖα, it is the unit that is the στοιχεῖον *par excellence,* since it furnishes οὐσία to the number that is generated, whereas the indefinite dyad acts as the ὕλη or δύναμις. The statements made regarding this latter mysterious conception are somewhat vague, and not always consistent, and it would appear that the Platonists held varying beliefs regarding it. In general, however, it may be said that it is the potentiality of quantity, of excess and defect. Some of the schools

called it δυοποιός[1], that which duplicates whatever
it operates upon, τοῦ γὰρ πολλὰ τὰ ὄντα εἶναι αἰτία
αὐτῆς ἡ φύσις[2]; and Simplicius adds: καθὸ γὰρ δυάς ἐστι,
πλῆθος καὶ ὀλιγότητα ἴσχεν ἐν ἑαυτῇ· καθὸ μὲν τὸ
διπλάσιόν ἐστιν, ἐν αὐτῇ πλῆθος...καθὸ δὲ ἥμισυ
ὀλιγότητα[3]. This tenet, however, was, I believe, the
result of a misconception regarding the origin of the
term δυάς, as will appear later. The ordinary phrase for
the δυάς, applied, we are told, in the first instance by
Plato, was τὸ μέγα καὶ τὸ μικρόν, but some Platonists preferred to call it by the general name πλῆθος[4]; whereas
others chose to employ a variant of the original μέγα
καὶ μικρὸν which seemed to them to be more appropriate
to the nature of the δυάς, viz., τὸ ὑπερέχον καὶ τὸ
ὑπερεχόμενον[5].

The third, Pythagorising, school need not detain us
long. Dropping all compromise, they maintained boldly
that things are numbers. To them possibly belonged
Xenocrates[6], who, interpreting p. 35 A of the Timaeus,
affirmed that the generation of the soul out of the
ἀμέριστος and the μεριστὴ οὐσία was simply the
generation of number out of ἓν and πλῆθος, and that
the soul was therefore only a number that moved itself;
and if we are to believe the account of Met. N. 5. 1092[b]
8 ff., there must have been very little to choose between
them and the Pythagoreans.

It is now time to turn to the consideration of the confused statements in Book A, with a view to determining

[1] M. 7. 1082 ᵃ 14; M. 8. 1083 ᵇ 36.
[2] M. 8. 1083 ᵃ 14.   [3] Simp. in Ar. Phys. 104 B.
[4] N. 1. 1087 ᵇ 30.   [5] N. 1. 1087 ᵇ 18.
[6] Ar. de An. A. 4. 408 ᵇ 32; Plutarch, περὶ τῆς ἐν Τιμαίῳ ψυχογονίας
c. 2.

how much of this number-doctrine can be legitimately fathered upon Plato, who is there said to have originated it. After various details regarding the ideas as originally described in the *Phaedo* and *Republic*, we are told that[1] Plato regarded the μαθηματικὰ as being μεταξὺ τῶν πραγμάτων, and apparently *at the same time* held that, since the εἴδη are the causes of ῥέοντα, their στοιχεῖα must accordingly be the στοιχεῖα of existing things also; and these στοιχεῖα were two, ὡς μὲν οὖν ὕλην τὸ μέγα καὶ τὸ μικρὸν εἶναι ἀρχάς, ὡς δ' οὐσίαν τὸ ἕν. This statement, on the face of it, proves that the writer was not careful to distinguish the different stages of Platonic doctrine. How could a belief in μαθηματικὰ as μεταξὺ between ideas and sensibles be held in conjunction with the doctrine that ideas are numbers composed of numerical στοιχεῖα? Our investigation of the two leading doctrines described in M and N showed us that the two positions were quite incompatible, inasmuch as the first school made their numbers ἀσύμβλητοι, whereas the latter made no such condition. A further confusion, moreover, is to be found in the phrase τὸ μέγα καὶ τὸ μικρὸν εἶναι ἀρχάς. According to N. 1. 1087 b 14, the view that made τὸ μέγα καὶ τὸ μικρὸν two separate ἀρχαὶ belonged to a very late sect of Plato's followers, and could not with accuracy be ascribed to him at all. The account of Plato's doctrine given here is, therefore, by no means clear or exact. The statement, however, that Plato made the ideas as numbers to consist of the ἓν and the μέγα καὶ μικρὸν is one that demands our attention, for it is borne out by other passages such as *Physics* Γ. 4. 203 ᵃ 10, Δ. 2. 209 ᵇ 33. But since Aristotle is so

[1] A. 6. 987 b 15.

lacking in precision concerning the divergences of the schools, and fails so often to point out where Plato ends and Platonism begins, the utmost caution must be exercised in attributing to Plato himself any of the number-doctrines mentioned by Aristotle, even when they bear his name. Only when we find confirmation in the dialogues themselves can we with certainty assume that Plato himself was the author of any of these views.

That Plato in the *Timaeus* has given to μαθηματικὰ an important place in his ideal reconstruction of the universe will not be denied by those who have accepted the results of Essays III and IV. Let us then compare τὸ μέγα καὶ τὸ μικρὸν of Aristotle's critique with the parallel conception in Plato, which was delineated first in the *Philebus* as τὸ μᾶλλόν τε καὶ ἧττον, and developed later into the χώρα of the *Timaeus*. Plato began, as we found in Essay II, with a realisation of the vast multitude of antithetical qualities in terms of which the flux of sense is for the most part to be expressed. The typical instances of these were τὸ θερμότερον καὶ ψυχρότερον, τὸ ξηρότερον καὶ ὑγρότερον, and τὸ μεῖζον καὶ σμικρότερον, the comparative degree marking the infinite variability of the attributes themselves and of the flux which they represented. The mere isolation of these qualities, however, from their environment seemed to imply the existence, κατὰ λόγον, at any rate, of something within which they arose and perished, and consequently we heard of ἡ τοῦ μᾶλλόν τε καὶ ἧττον ἕδρα, within which the antithetical qualities found a home, that which made their existence possible. In the *Timaeus* we found the conception of the ἕδρα still further developed; Plato there, in fact, had sketched[1] for us in clear language the abstract notion of space, within which these qualities arise, together with the objects which they compose (τὸ δὲ ὁποιονοῦν τι, θερμὸν ἢ λευκὸν ἢ καὶ ὁτιοῦν τῶν ἐναντίων καὶ πάνθ' ὅσα ἐκ τούτων). Plato also had utilised this conception in order to give an intelligible representation of the ideas of natural objects; within this abstract χώρα he caused to appear the ideal counterparts of fire, air, earth and water—geometrical structures composed of triangles combined in various proportions, the highest expression of the eternal laws of Becoming.

Now it is extremely probable that the phrase ἀόριστος δυάς, so much used by Aristotle, arose while the theory of space was taking shape, and was based on the description in the *Philebus*, in which we are presented with the picture of two extremes in ever-varying degrees of approximation to, and divergence from, each other. The writer of N practically acknowledges this when he speaks of ἡ τοῦ ἀνίσου δυὰς τοῦ μεγάλου καὶ μικροῦ[2]. If the phrase had originated as an arithmetical term simply, i.e., as the equivalent of the duplicating force, it would not have been conjoined invariably with those two antithetical adjectives. Moreover, when Plato's analysis of matter developed still further and was found to consist ultimately in the notion of abstract space, it is quite conceivable that the χώρα, the δύναμις or ὕλη of size and extension, should be popularly described in the school by the ἀόριστος δυὰς most appropriate to it,

---

[1] *Tim.* 50 A.   [2] N. 1. 1087 b 7.

viz., that of τὸ μεῖζον καὶ σμικρότερον or τὸ μέγα καὶ
τὸ μικρόν; for the tendency of the *Timaeus* was to
make all these sensible qualities but variations of the
fundamental opposition of τὸ μέγα καὶ τὸ μικρόν, as
the exposition of 61 E ff. particularly shows. The
qualities of hot and cold, hard and soft, and the like,
are dependent upon the geometrical structure of the
elements which produce them; they are secondary
effects[1] of the primary differences of shape in the
elementary figures, and consequently τὸ μέγα καὶ τὸ
μικρὸν is the fundamental opposition of matter. But,
after the date of the *Timaeus*, while the Platonic
number-theory was rapidly developing in various di-
rections, the phrase τὸ μέγα καὶ τὸ μικρὸν undoubtedly
came to be used in a somewhat restricted sense, and in
a fashion that to the writer of M and N appeared
inaccurate. It was applied to the ὕλη of ἀριθμοὶ as
such, which to many contemporary Platonists[2] seemed
to be represented better by the words τὸ πολὺ καὶ
τὸ ὀλίγον, or τὸ ὑπερέχον καὶ τὸ ὑπερεχόμενον. Some
indeed repudiated τὸ μέγα καὶ τὸ μικρὸν altogether,
and substituted the simpler πλῆθος. All, however,
agreed in making the ἓν the other στοιχεῖον, and regarding it as the source of οὐσία in the numbers that
were generated.

Now is there any indication that Plato himself was
responsible for this extension of the phrase τὸ μέγα καὶ
τὸ μικρόν? In c. 6 of Book A, previously referred to,
he is not only said to have employed it in this way,
but the reasons for his doing so are given in a passage
that abounds in reminiscences of the *Timaeus*. "The

---

[1] Cf. M. 9. 1085 ᵃ 10.   [2] N. 1. 1087 ᵇ 16 ff.

second στοιχεῖον," says Aristotle[1], "they made a dyad, because the numbers, with the exception of the πρῶτοι ἀριθμοί (i.e., the ideas of numbers advocated by the first of the Platonic sects), were easily generated out of it, as it were from an ἐκμαγεῖον." "And yet," Aristotle goes on to say, "the Platonic account is not in harmony with facts, for in actual life one εἶδος generates many things out of many substances, not from one ὕλη, as the Platonists say; neither is their simile of the father and the mother consistent with their doctrine." Here we have obviously the argument and the imagery of *Timaeus* 50 A—E reproduced in a condensed form, and transferred from the conception of χώρα, to which they were originally applied, to that of a δύναμις of plurality, out of which, with the aid of the unit, ἀριθμοὶ are evolved. Not only, then, may we suppose the existence of a χώρα, within which all manner of geometrical figures are generated, but even the more select science of number must have as its foundation a conception of an arithmetical ὕλη, an arithmetical ἄπειρον, from which, with the aid of the "atomic" unit, the whole army of numbers is to be created.

This extension of geometrical terms to the science of number is by no means surprising. It was the recognised scientific method of the day. From the first geometry had been called into requisition to exemplify the technical differences of number, as the mathematical demonstration of the *Theaetetus*[2] clearly indicates. If the square, the oblong and the gnomon[3]

---

[1] A. 6. 987 b 33.   [2] *Theaet.* 147 D seq.
[3] Cf. Ar. *Phys.* Γ. 4. 203 a 14.

each represented a mathematical principle which is
valid for the science of number, no less than that of
surface, why should not the abstract, ideal χώρα,
within which these figures arise, also have its counterpart in arithmetic? What is it that makes the generation of number possible? The point, which forms
the original basis of all superficial and solid figures,
is, in arithmetic, the unit, the στιγμὴ ἄθετος[1]. The
χώρα, or the μέγα καὶ μικρόν, then, of number, is that
which provides for the multiplication, the pluralisation
of the unit, the vague δύναμις of amplification, of
quantity, which is best described as τὸ ὑπερέχον καὶ
τὸ ὑπερεχόμενον[2].

It is not at all incredible that Plato may have been
the author of this development in mathematical science,
but it is more difficult to believe that he associated it
with his ideal theory of numbers, and said that the
mathematical ἕν and the ἀόριστος δυὰς of number
were the στοιχεῖα of the ideas and all existing things,
as Aristotle indicates. In Essay IV we had reason to
believe that in the *Timaeus* he posited the existence
of certain mathematical ideas—the mathematical laws
which governed the existence of all perceptible things,
and which, for him, represented their truest reality,
inasmuch as they were the eternal and intelligible
counterparts of the things of flux. But these laws of
matter depended for their expression on geometrical,
no less than arithmetical, formulae. The science of
number, indeed, supplied the proportions which were
necessary to the formulation of the law; number was
in a manner its οὐσία, but the no less essential ὕλη

[1] M. 8. 1084 b 26.   [2] Cf. Ar. *Phys.* Γ. 6. 206 b 27.

128   THE ARISTOTELIAN CRITIQUE OF

took the form of primary geometrical triangles, in-
volving, of course, the μέγα καὶ μικρὸν of space. And
some Platonists seem to have adhered to this view to
the end, if we can trust the evidence of M. 9. 1085 ᵃ 33,
where it is stated that some preferred to think of the
ideas as composed of the στιγμὴ and a spatial ὕλη.
It is just possible, however, that Plato may have
analysed the στοιχεῖα of his mathematical ideas yet
further, and announced that the ultimate elements of
all were the numerical unit and the numerical ἀόριστος
δυάς. At N. 3. 1090 ᵇ 21 the adherents of the second
school of Platonism are represented as generating
mathematical μεγέθη (which are the equivalent of the
mathematical ideas of the *Timaeus*) out of ἀριθμὸς and
ὕλη, through their identification of the point with the
unit, and so on, and deriving number itself from the ἓν
and the ἀόριστος δυὰς as ἀρχαί. Moreover, it is quite
conceivable that Plato would have concurred in the
view, given at B. 1002 ᵃ 4, that the surface is prior to the
solid, the line to the surface, and the point and monad
to the line. Seeing, therefore, that Plato in all probability *did* regard[1] the fundamental conceptions of
geometry as varieties of the corresponding arithmetical
notions, by his identification of the point with unity,
the line with duality, and so on, it may be that he
finally decided that the ultimate bases of the mathematical ideas were the unit and the arithmetical μέγα
καὶ μικρόν. Some such modification of view is declared
by Aristotle in his *Physics* to have taken place. In the
fourth book of the *Physics*[2] we are told that Plato's

---

[1] See *Rep.* 528 A, B.   Cf. *Phys.* Γ. 6. 206 ᵇ 27.

[2] *Phys.* Δ. 2. 209 ᵇ 11.

account of ὕλη, or τὸ μεταληπτικόν, in the *Timaeus* was different from that given in the ἄγραφα δόγματα: διὸ καὶ Πλάτων τὴν ὕλην καὶ τὴν χώραν ταὐτό φησιν εἶναι ἐν τῷ Τιμαίῳ· τὸ γὰρ μεταληπτικὸν καὶ τὴν χώραν ἓν καὶ ταὐτόν, ἄλλον δὲ τρόπον ἐκεῖ τε λέγων τὸ μεταληπτικὸν καὶ ἐν τοῖς λεγομένοις ἀγράφοις δόγμασιν. Similar affirmations from other commentators on Plato or Aristotle are too numerous to mention. If these considerations, then, are to be accepted as proof, we may say that Plato's own later views are to be assigned, if to any, to the second of the Platonic schools which we have been considering.

We may then, I think, regard it as certain that Plato, in his latest stage, paid great attention to certain mathematical ideas, or laws, governing material existences, and as highly probable that he proved these mathematical proportions to be capable of being analysed into two ultimate elements, the ἕν and the indefinite dyad. Immediately after his death, however, and possibly before, the Platonists seem to have fastened on the number-theory as a fit medium for all manner of Pythagorean extravagances, which the philosophical Plato could not have entertained for a moment. This they accomplished partly by amalgamating with the number-doctrine certain Pythagorean traditions, such as the attribution of special virtue[1] to the numbers ten or seven, and the derivation of good and evil from the ultimate πέρας and ἄπειρον in number, and partly by interpreting certain passages in Plato's dialogues in too literal a sense. It would seem, in fact, that a regular school for the interpretation of the dialogues started

[1] See N. 6. 1093ᵃ 28; M. 8. 1084ᵃ 12; N. 4. 1091ᵇ 34.

w. 9

soon after Plato's death. Xenocrates' interpretation of *Timaeus* 35 A has already been touched upon; and the wide-spread view that the δυάς was the cause of evil, and the ἕν consequently of good, was in all probability based upon passages like *Timaeus* 53 B, where the ὑποδοχή, before the introduction of method and measure, is said to have been the reverse of κάλλιστον and ἄριστον. The combination of the ideas of the *Republic* with the number-theory, as illustrated in the doctrine of the first school of Platonists, is also a case in point. Moreover, the people[1] who fancifully attributed the number one to νοῦς, two to ἐπιστήμη, three to δόξα, and so on, were probably interpreting the *Timaeus* in a fashion of their own. The principle that soul is composed of the same elements as the things upon which it operates, which Plato presumably enunciated in his story of the creation of ψυχή out of Same, Other, etc., gave rise to the inference that αἴσθησις, like the αἰσθητόν, is represented by the number 4, whence, by Pythagorean analogy, the numbers one, two, three, were assigned to the other activities of soul.

Such, then, is the sum of the information to be obtained from Aristotle's critique. In the course of our enquiry we have found confirmation for the belief that Plato's ideal theory changed its character from time to time according as his knowledge, and particularly his logical knowledge, grew, that, although for him the assumption of eternal ideas was always obligatory, he latterly no longer retained them for the explanation of things whose mystery was easily solved by the logic of ordinary intelligence, and that his account of the idea

[1] *De An.* A. 2. 404 ᵇ 20.

at the end of his life was materially different from that of the *Phaedo* and the *Republic*. In Essays III and IV we had reason to think that, at the end of his days, he recognised two distinct classes of ideal existences, the first being at once the eternal cause of all Becoming and the ethical ideal of every living soul, the second being a mathematical law governing material bodies, the direct criterion of physical beauty. Of the former Aristotle takes no account; but from his exhaustive treatment of the latter it would appear that the mathematical ideas, being the more tangible, took the fancy of the school, and attracted greater investigation. And our conclusion that these mathematical ideas were restricted to natural objects only, to the exclusion of qualities, relations, σκευαστά and such-like, has found abundant confirmation in Aristotle's own words. It has also become clear that the nature of the ideas, as they were conceived successively in such dialogues as the *Sophist*, *Philebus*, and *Timaeus*, was not in the least comprehended by Aristotle, since he expects them to be in every respect identical with those of the *Phaedo* and the *Republic*, and complains when he discovers that they are not. The only phase of the ideal theory on which he can speak with any confidence is the very latest stage, the doctrine of numbers, and even there, as we saw in our examination of A. c. 6, he is not careful to distinguish between Plato's own view, and those which are elsewhere acknowledged to be subsequent accretions.

To follow Aristotle in detail through his criticisms of Plato and the Platonic point of view would be an unprofitable as well as a tedious task, for nearly every objection is levelled from the author's scientific point of view, and with an idealist would have no weight at all. The scorn which is heaped upon the ideas in general is directed largely against the metaphorical processes of μέθεξις and μίμησις[1], which Plato used in describing their functions; as Plato himself would have acknowledged these to be mere μεταφοραὶ ποιητικοί, the criticism is hardly useful. The ideas as numbers are chiefly criticised because they imply the priority of ἀριθμός[2], which is a συμβεβηκός, to the σύνολον, which is οὐσία. This taunt is, of course, dependent upon Aristotle's classification of categories, in which οὐσία precedes ποσόν—which is scarcely a fit criterion to use in reviewing a predecessor, whose whole point of view was opposed to such a classification. Another objection consists in the statement that, even if the idea *is* a number[3], it must be ἀριθμὸς τινῶν, of some material ingredients—which in itself shows how materialistic was Aristotle's point of view, and how utterly he had failed to grasp the subtlety of Plato's speculations in the *Timaeus*. There are a few points, indeed, which might justly be made by any man of science, but the criticism on the whole is so absurdly literal that it scarcely merits serious reading. The attack[4] on the δυὰς ἀόριστος, for instance, is based largely on the notion that it is literally a dyad, which we know to be inaccurate. In fact, Aristotle is the last authority to look to for a fair and liberal account of Platonism.

---

[1] A. 9. 991ᵃ 10, 20 ; M. 5. 1079ᵇ 25.
[2] B. 5. 1001ᵇ 26 ; M. 9. 1085ᵃ 20.
[3] A. 9. 991ᵇ 20 ; N. 5. 1092ᵇ 22.
[4] M. 7. 1081ᵇ 17 ; 8. 1084ᵇ 37.

Under these circumstances there was, of course, little likelihood that Plato's system, especially in its latest form, should be handed down to us in the form in which he himself evolved and formulated it. Everything has tended to obscure both the expression and the content of the number-theory, and one may almost agree with Berkeley, and say that "Aristotle and his followers have made a monstrous representation of the Platonic ideas, and some of Plato's own school have said very odd things concerning them[1]." The aim of this paper has been to show that, in spite of all these obscurations, one can detect a certain residuum that may fairly be ascribed to Plato himself, and that the number-theory cannot be summed up placidly as an elaborate fiction concocted by Plato's successors for the mere purpose of deceiving posterity.

[1] Berkeley, *Reflexions and Inquiries*, § 338. (Bohn's edition vol. iii. p. 325.)

For EU product safety concerns, contact us at Calle de José Abascal, 56–1°,
28003 Madrid, Spain or eugpsr@cambridge.org.

www.ingramcontent.com/pod-product-compliance
Ingram Content Group UK Ltd.
Pitfield, Milton Keynes, MK11 3LW, UK
UKHW020314140625
459647UK00018B/1862